Endorseme

"Pay attention to Kevin's journey through what it is like for a diverse society to coexist with harmony and respect as he personally has a unique perspective from a white and black perspective. He helps expose why we can not relax if we want our society to continue to make progress for our children and their children."

James P Hackett
Former President and CEO of Ford Motor Company and Steelcase, Inc.

"*The Multiethnic Advantage* is an outstanding resource for fostering multiethnicity in the workplace! The author presents an engaging and practical approach to understanding its importance and offers realistic, sensible, and strategic methods to get started. Additionally, the book effectively addresses many of the common concerns companies have about embracing multiethnicity by providing practical solutions."

Julie MacFarland
President, JL HR Consulting
Former Regional Manager, Career Development Center
Regional Manager Talent Acquisition, Trinity Health

"In an era where misinformation has led to distorted thinking about the value of having diverse people in an organization. Kevin Heyne has developed in this book a practical guide to strengthening your organization by having diverse opinions coming from many different people. This book builds the case that differences bring added dimensions and strengthen companies and organizations not only because it is the right thing to do but because it assures their longevity and effectiveness. *The Multiethnic Advantage* walks leadership through a step-by-step process of engaging people who come from different backgrounds in order to ensure a thriving culture. This is a must-read for anyone interested in the journey to achieve a multiethnic culture in their organization."

Fred Keller
Founder of Cascade Engineering
Former chair of the US Department of Commerce
Manufacturing Council

"This book is not propagating some political agenda, nor is it pushing shame on leaders for a lack of diversity in their ranks. Rather, Kevin's ability to get to the point in a very personal, common sense, and practical way makes this a must-read for any of today's business or organizational leaders. Just as leadership is practiced, *The Multiethnic Advantage* lays out timeless practices for leaders desiring to innovate and be relevant in this ever-changing and multiethnic world."

Dr. Justin Beene
Entrepreneur, Visionary, and
Founder of an innovative partnership
The Grand Rapids Center for Community Transformation

"I have worked with Kevin over the past 5 years since he joined Lumbermen's, and his book *The Multiethnic Advantage* represents Kevin's passion and commitment to multiethnic diversity. The book articulates the transformative power of a multiethnic workforce, offering insights and best practices that are both practical and impactful. As businesses continue to recognize the value of diversity, this book serves as a roadmap to not just starting the journey but sustaining meaningful change."

Andrew Korzen
President & CEO
Wilsonart Engineered Surfaces

"Dr. Kevin Heyne's *The Multiethnic Advantage* is a must-read for anyone serious about cultivating a dynamic and inclusive company culture. Packed with powerful personal stories, practical tools, and sharp insights, this book makes an undeniable case for the transformative impact of embracing multiethnic diversity in the workplace. If you're ready to unlock your organization's full potential, this is the guide you've been waiting for."

Steve Sanders
Vice President Global Operations
Steelcase, Inc.

"*The Multi-Ethnic Advantage* is a must-read for anyone committed to fostering a more inclusive workplace. Kevin masterfully weaves in his personal journey, offering a unique perspective on the power of racial and ethnic diversity. His insights on employee engagement and practical best practices make this book not only inspiring but also a valuable resource for any leader looking to elevate their organization."

Ovell Barbee
HR Strategist and owner of Ovell Rome and Associates,
"Ask Ovell" and author of *The Big House*
Former HR Executive, CHRO, & Chief Diversity Officer
Held leadership roles at Motorola, GM, Blue Cross,
Corewell Health, and Indiana University Health System

"For those of us who want to leave a legacy impacted by *The Multiethnic Advantage*, regardless of the type of organization we are leading, Dr. Heyne has provided us with an excellent resource for just that. This book provides the inspiration and motivation to take the critical 'first steps' and a blueprint to move your multiethnic vision to a manifested real-life, tangible reality! As Dr. Heyne says, 'Your offspring will be the inheritors of what we're creating today.'"

Eric D. Brown
President and CEO
Urban League of West Michigan

"*The Multiethnic Advantage: Elevating Your Organization through Racial and Ethnic Diversity* is an insightful and practical guide for leaders committed to creating more inclusive and innovative organizations. Through a structured, step-by-step approach, Kevin clearly outlines the 'why,' the 'how,' and the best practices needed to embed diversity into the fabric of an organization. As someone who drives sales effectiveness in a competitive manufacturing industry, I appreciate the book's emphasis on vision, ownership, and employee engagement, which are crucial for any company's success. The real-world case study and actionable insights make this a must-read for leaders ready to apply these principles and gain a lasting advantage. This is the roadmap for those ready to make meaningful progress on their diversity journey—start today!"

Elsa Sanchez
Director of Commercial Sales Effectiveness

"Kevin takes on a very complex topic at a time when one could easily be tempted to think that it's 'just one of those...'. Having originated from a country with a multicultural setting, I can attest firsthand to the benefits of having a diverse team, not because it's a trend but because it presents the basis for a robust team and, beyond that, the foundation for the good of society at large. The reality is Kevin presented a real and reflective case based on lived experiences and an authenticity that gives much credence to the facts outlined in his book while delivering practical suggestions. A must-read for all levels, especially leaders!"

Kevin Suraj
Order Fulfillment Leader
Steelcase, Inc.

"This book is a powerful guide for leaders committed to building truly inclusive and diverse organizations, offering practical strategies grounded in vision, data-driven processes, and grace-filled employee engagement. It's an essential resource for anyone passionate about fostering unity and equity in the workplace and beyond."

Artie M. Lindsay Sr.
Pastor of Spiritual Formation,
Tabernacle Community Church

"In a world where multiethnic diversity remains elusive for many organizations, this book offers a refreshingly honest and practical approach to making it a reality. Through candid interviews and thoughtful insights, the author reveals that while the journey is challenging, it's far from impossible. By highlighting examples like Cascade Engineering and

Trinity Health, we see that lasting change is possible when leadership commits to the long haul. This book is an essential read for any leader who wants to foster a truly inclusive and diverse organization—and is willing to put in the work to get there."

Marylu Villarreal
Operations Group Manager
Monterey, Mexico
Steelcase, Inc.

"The world is changing. The largest migration of human beings in the history of the world is currently taking place through migration from country to country and from rural areas to cities. Healthy organizations can adjust and thrive amidst these circumstances by intentionally establishing multiethnic organizations. Kevin Heyne's book is a helpful tool to guide the way for leaders who are interested in remaining relevant and making an impact in today's multicultural world. His personal life, combined with his local community impact, experience interacting with faith-based organizations, and business world expertise, have yielded practical guidelines based on his own innovative research that will deliver results over time. I highly recommend this resource!"

Dr. Bryan McCabe
President
Bakke Graduate University

"I have known Kevin for almost twenty years. I have lived with him in church life and on the softball diamond. The one thing I love about Kevin is his humility and authenticity. He has encouraged and challenged me in so many ways. So, when he asked me to read and comment on his new book, I felt honored. *The Multiethnic Advantage: Elevating Your Organization through Racial and Ethnic Diversity* is an insightful and practical guide for organizations seeking to embrace diversity and inclusion. Kevin expertly outlines best practices for building and sustaining a multiethnic organization, emphasizing diversity's strategic and relational benefits. The book is not about white guilt but is rich with actionable advice, making it a valuable resource for leaders at any stage of their diversity journey. Dr. Heyne challenges organizations to go beyond surface-level diversity efforts and cultivate a truly inclusive culture. I highly recommend this gem."

Marvin Williams
Lead Pastor
Trinity Church

"*The Multiethnic Advantage* is both a crash course and masterclass of practical wisdom and insightful understanding. It illustrates in equal measure both the challenges and opportunities of leading a diverse organization. In addition to the professional tools offered in this book, Kevin sprinkles in poignant stories from his personal journey to underline its truth."

Julian Newman
CEO, Futurecast Foundation
Founder/CEO, Culture Creative
Author of *Beautiful Together*

"It is my pleasure to endorse Dr. Kevin Heyne's literary work entitled *The Multiethnic Advantage*. This book is a roadmap that will guide your organization in how to intentionally move your workforce toward multiethnicity. In doing so, you'll maximize creativity, innovation, and strategic insight. I appreciate Dr. Heyne's lived experience, which is critically important and gives his comments credibility. Also, Dr. Heyne is absolutely correct when he identifies Vision and Ownership as the most important ingredient in doing this work effectively."

Cle J. Jackson
President, NAACP Greater Grand Rapids Branch

"An engaging and accessible must-read for all business leaders! Study after study has confirmed that organizations with multi-ethnic workforces are more likely to outperform their less diverse competitors. *The Multiethnic Advantage* provides a proven and easy-to-follow framework for driving positive change at your company. As an Association leader who has worked with a number of different industries, I know that attracting and retaining talent is an ongoing challenge for businesses of all sizes. Building a team that reflects the increasingly diverse B2B and B2C landscape is a competitive advantage in the near term and an absolute necessity in the long term. Author Kevin Heyne succinctly outlines the 'why' and 'how,' you just need to get started."

Michael Wilbur
Executive Director of NBMDA and NAFCD

THE MULTIETHNIC ADVANTAGE

ELEVATING YOUR ORGANIZATION THROUGH RACIAL AND ETHNIC DIVERSITY: BEST PRACTICES TO START AND SUSTAIN YOUR JOURNEY

THE MULTIETHNIC ADVANTAGE

ELEVATING YOUR ORGANIZATION THROUGH RACIAL AND ETHNIC DIVERSITY: BEST PRACTICES TO START AND SUSTAIN YOUR JOURNEY

DR. KEVIN HEYNE

ethos
collective

Printed in the United States of America

Published by Igniting Souls
PO Box 43, Powell, OH 43065
IgnitingSouls.com

LCCN: 2024911287
Paperback ISBN: 978-1-63680-316-6
Hardcover ISBN: 978-1-63680-317-3
e-book ISBN: 978-1-63680-318-0

Available in paperback, hardcover, e-book, and audiobook.

Any Internet addresses (websites, blogs, etc.) and telephone numbers printed in this book are offered as a resource. They are not intended in any way to be or imply an endorsement by Igniting Souls, nor does Igniting Souls vouch for the content of these sites and numbers for the life of this book.

Some names and identifying details may have been changed to protect the privacy of individuals.

Dedication

To my mom and dad, whose unwavering respect for all people inspired my own values. The value you placed on every human being has impacted my life in a significant way.

To the love of my life, Lynne, whose insight, encouragement, and belief in me helped this book become a reality. I'm indebted to your challenge to go deeper and to your inspiration to be a difference-maker in our world.

To Ethan, Colin, Chelsea, Brandon, and precious Giuliana, you are deeply loved and have much to offer humanity. Go for the dreams you've been created to pursue!

When the righteous prosper, the city rejoices.
—Proverbs 11:10

Contents

Foreword

When I first began discussing with Dr. Kevin Heyne the possibility of him joining the leadership team at Lumbermen's, I couldn't have predicted the impact that eventual hiring decision would have on our corporate culture. In those initial exchanges, Kevin asked about my position on racial diversity and the company's approach to becoming more multiethnic. I didn't realize at the time that these early conversations would come to represent the start of a challenging but amazing path.

Seeking greater racial diversity is challenging for leadership in any setting due to the emotions and preconceptions surrounding this topic. The heated debate around Critical Race Theory alone is enough to scare leaders away from tackling this important issue. Fortunately for us, Kevin came to Lumbermen's with a life of experience and a Doctorate of Transformational Leadership, with much of his research focused on achieving greater multiethnicity within all types of organizations. The concepts presented in this book reflect Kevin's practical steps in leading our company toward greater ethnic diversity.

Lumbermen's roots go back to 1955 when three brothers—Paul, John, and Henry Bouma—formed a building material supply company in the housing-starved post-war era. The business grew quickly, adding more employees as the years went on. From the beginning, the Bouma family created a legacy of caring for their employees and the community.

Fast-forward a couple of decades, and care for employees and the community still defines us. But in 2017, we became very purposeful about defining our brand and culture, a process that led to a restated Mission, Vision, and set of Promises to guide our actions. Our stated mission became: "We exist to enrich the lives of people by intentionally caring for all who experience us."

Against this backdrop, Kevin joined Lumbermen's in 2019, and he hit the "start" button on our quest for greater multiethnicity and our desire to cultivate a valuable experience for all people of color within our organization. The initial step on this racial diversity path was to raise awareness, first with our leadership team and then with all employee-owners.

Once I came to understand the bias and outright discrimination that existed in the very post-war housing expansion from which Lumbermen's was born, I personally moved from being "on board" with a commitment to change to becoming passionate about it. While I firmly believe that Lumbermen's was not complicit, its founding on the south side of Grand Rapids during a period when many suburban communities were being developed as a result of urban flight—and recognizing that this housing boom was deeply intertwined with discrimination—struck a chord with me and further accelerated our multiethnic efforts. A case study detailing these efforts can be found in Chapter 6 of the book.

In Chapter 1, Kevin asks, "What will practically help an organization progress in becoming multiethnic?" The subsequent pages capture many valuable thoughts on this topic. In fact, for those who are unsure of where to even begin, Kevin's book serves as a first-rate blueprint for how to practically cultivate racial and ethnic diversity in a positive way. One of the key principles in achieving this is through leadership buy-in. I have already mentioned that my "Aha!" moment came from heightened awareness that racism has a recent history in our country, that it still exists today, and that the ripple effects are pervasive throughout society.

Kevin begins his book by identifying the importance of understanding our WHY. There are many "whys" to pursuing a more multiethnic organization, but for me, it is simply the right thing to do. What is your why? Reading this book can help unlock those answers and start you on the journey toward cultivating your "multiethnic advantage."

Steve Petersen
President/CEO, Lumbermen's, Inc.

Introduction:
An Invitation to a Positive
Way Forward

There I sat, proud to share the room with the top movers and shakers of a global Fortune 1000 company. I was thrilled to be part of this elite group, which was assigned to the monumental task of planning initiatives that would impact the future of our business. But as my eyes traveled around the room, I was jarred by a stinging reality: almost everyone present was white. This giant of an industry had gathered its *crème de la crème*, high-level leaders pulling down six figures-plus annually, to decide how best to serve our diverse customer base; yet, of the 70-plus attendees, only two, maybe three, people of color had a seat at the table.

Scenes like this continue to play out across the United States, even with all of the attention around diversity, equity, and inclusion (DEI) in recent years. In fact, I write this book at a time when the world is deeply conflicted about the DEI movement, with some saying we desperately need it and others arguing that it desperately needs to disappear.

When it comes to the topic of race in America, the differences in opinion are often staggering. For example, here are a few sample statements made by people of color that reflect frustration with the ongoing battle over racial justice and what is perceived to be a blindness to the issue:

"White people don't get it!"
"Racism is real, and they keep dismissing it!"
"America needs a wake-up call and quick!"

On the other hand, many white people are exhausted by the topic and make statements like:

"Aren't we done with this conversation?!"
"This was addressed in the 60's, so let's get over it! Continuing this conversation only makes matters worse!"
"I'm so tired of the media fanning the flames of an issue that was dealt with years ago!"

These are generalizations, of course. I recognize that not everyone who is white shares the above sentiments, nor does every person of color feel the exact same way about the issue. There are white people who insist on making real change. And there are people of color who push back against the detriments of any initiative or training that might lead to a victim mindset. Opinions are all over the map. If one were to rate it as a topic needing attention on a scale of 1 to 10, one group might give it a 1 or a 2, while another might give it a 9 or a 10. We must think through this carefully, but if we're honest with ourselves, it's quite evident there's plenty of room for improvement. It isn't about victimhood, "white guilt," or getting stuck in the past—it's about recognizing our history for what it is and focusing our energy on solutions—and that's what I want us to explore. At the end of the day, it's about taking leadership of an important issue of our time.

I am a white male who grew up in the suburbs of four major cities (more on this later). My wife is African American, and we have three biracial children. My lived experience over the years informs my knowledge on this subject. Since childhood, I have been in numerous conversations on the topic of race and racism and have an understanding of the different sides of this issue.

For nearly 30 years, I have held high-level leadership roles at three top-notch organizations and have attempted to encourage multiethnic diversity in all of them. I am a practitioner who longs to implement best practices that make an organization better. I recognize that I don't have all the answers, but do believe that I have an important contribution to make and am in a unique position to speak to this topic, as I'm impacted by it personally as well as professionally. So, I write this book for leaders of any organization as a practical way forward to help bridge this ethnic gap and make your organization that much better.

The message contained in this book is for leaders of any ethnicity, but it certainly speaks loudest to those who are white. That's who's often in the room making these decisions and who will need to spearhead multiethnic change. At the same time, there are many people of color in leadership who are looking for better ways to implement this type of change, so this book is for you as well. Finally, it's also written for the non-leader who has a passion for seeing multiethnicity lived out in the workplace.

Data...

What does the data say? It's certainly true that since the 1960s and the Civil Rights legislation, people of color have seen great progress. The poverty rate in this population has declined[1], the share of people getting a college degree has increased,[2] and there's much greater representation in Congress.[3] Yet, wage and household income disparity between whites and other races remains significant.[4] And what about the workplace?

Whether you're in a small or large organization, chances are you'll find significantly more white people than people of color in the professional ranks. According to 2023 data from the U.S. Bureau of Labor Statistics,[5] 76.9% of whites reside in management, professional, and related occupations. Although African Americans and Latinos comprise 31.6% of the overall employed population, they make up only 21.8% of management, professional, and related occupations, which is statistically significant. In other words, in order to achieve the same representation of African Americans and Latinos in the management and professional ranks that is found in the overall employed population, there would need to be a 45% increase! Additionally, while 85.8% of chief executives are white (a much greater percentage than the white employed population), only 5.2% of executives are African American (a much lower percentage than the African-American employed population).

In Kent County, Michigan, where I reside, despite representing 78% of the population, white residents own 95% of the businesses and earn 98% of the total revenue.[6] The reality is this: the percentage of people of color in the professional and leadership ranks is frequently much lower than the percentage found in an organization's surrounding communities.

You might be thinking, "So? As long as you have good people working here, why should their skin color matter?" It's an understandable question in a society that prides itself on equality and meritocracy. In principle, skin color should not matter. In reality, skin color *does* matter, as our biases—unconscious or not—often impact who is hired and who gets promoted. Even in some of the most well-meaning organizations, a person's pigmentation can affect how much they earn, how high they climb—and how well the organization serves its customers.

Skin color also matters because of the shrinking size of the overall US white population. In 1960, the white population was 88.6%. In 2023, this number was 75.5%.[7] Over the next decade, it will plummet even further. To cap it off, while interracial marriage was only 3% in 1967, according to the Pew Research Center, this number rose to 19% in 2019[8]. The browning of America is a real trend that will continue to happen in years to come.

Given the disparity that still exists in the professional and leadership ranks of the workforce, why is it so hard for the well-intentioned leader to press forward with this topic? Often, the response is found in some sort of DEI program, but for various reasons, some of these haven't produced the desired results. Additionally, a fair amount of controversy often surrounds these initiatives, so who wants to add another challenge when there's so much else to tackle?

How...

The question of our day is: How do we address this issue in a fresh and productive way? How do we move from an off-the-shelf "program" mentality to a way of operating that is built into the DNA of our organization? How do we move

from our tribalism regarding this topic—surrounding ourselves with people who are like us—to a place where "like
us" encompasses all ethnicities? And... how do we move to
a way of life that holistically addresses our organization's
attraction and retention practices so that all ethnicities are
valued equally?

It's time to start viewing this differently. Despite the dis-
sonance surrounding this topic, it's not something to move
away from but embrace for the good of our organization. You
don't have to start a new program as much as cultivate an
organizational way of life that weaves itself into the fabric of
your organization. Here's the beauty of it: if done well, this
will create a positive climate for all employees.

I have my own personal journey and pain surrounding
this topic. I suspect most white people are like a rubber band
that snaps back to its original shape when the conversation
is over and are able to go on with their lives, never having to
think about it again. In my case, I live with the topic daily,
have been hurt by people's responses at times, and sometimes
feel like I'm alone on an island. For all of these reasons, I
was compelled to embark on a doctoral dissertation focused
on identifying best practices that move an organization forward in embracing and valuing all ethnicities. This book is a
summary of my research that will help you as a leader understand what it takes to grow your organization in ways never
thought possible.

What am I proposing? I'm proposing that you tailor
these ideas to your organization. Every entity is different,
so think through what you can do to weave this into your
organizational fabric. It's critical that it aligns with your
organizational values, which hopefully speak to creating a
better workplace for all. In order to do this, I'd like you to
consider the following:

1. Recognize the historical reality of what has transpired in our country regarding race and ethnicity and better understand why the effects are still lingering today.

2. Given the context of this historical reality, understand how bias affects us and plays itself out in the workplace.

3. Re-tool your attraction and retention systems to ensure they're designed to value all ethnicities equally.

4. Develop more relationships with people of different ethnicities so that "like us" includes people who are different from us. Recognize how similar we are in our humanity. As Maya Angelou once said, "We are more alike than we are unalike!"[9]

Ultimately, it is a heart issue. We may overlook or downplay this truth, but when we do, it's to our own peril. The 1960s Civil Rights legislation may have changed the law, but it didn't necessarily change people's hearts. Laws are designed to promote good behavior, which is important. But heart change happens at the speed of deep relationships. It happens one relationship at a time as we build trust and connection when rubbing shoulders with each other.

What if...

What if we decided to pursue a more multiethnic organization? What if we chose to open ourselves up to the many benefits that come from people with different backgrounds and experiences working together? Multiethnic diversity offers a richness that many organizations never experience. Think of the wholeness found in having a team comprised of different personalities. This is only enhanced by adding multiethnicity.

A thriving multiethnic environment accomplishes several outcomes. For one, it builds a stronger culture and makes the organization healthier as people learn from others with different backgrounds. Additionally, it allows you to tap into a larger talent pool, ensuring you select the best people possible for your organization. Given today's labor challenges, this alone is compelling enough. But it also achieves something more that's quite powerful: it brings people together who've long been divided, and it builds relationships between people who've held deep-rooted biases towards each other. Bridges are built, relationships are formed, and opinions are rethought when different ethnicities come together. True heart change takes place as one human being is touched by another. All of humanity is uplifted as people who've been separated are now working closely together.

Okay, I know not everyone is here for a "kumbaya" moment, but I'm speaking from experience. When we cultivate a healthy multiethnic environment, we literally change lives as people form new relationships and begin dismantling acquired stereotypes. The result is a workplace culture that is more rich, robust, and resilient.

There are people who would contribute and add value to your organization—value that you are currently overlooking—if you only understood how to reach them. Until recently, most organizations had simply never thought about this topic. It's probably still true that most organizations don't think it's important and take little action to address it. As our economy becomes increasingly global and our country increasingly diverse, organizations that don't prize multiethnicity will eventually find themselves losing relevance.

But even if you're one of those leaders who recognize this reality and want to do something about it, you likely don't know exactly what to do. You want to broaden your employee base and strengthen your culture but have limited know-how. Past actions to become more multiethnic never went anywhere; the momentum dried up, and you effectively abandoned the idea altogether.

Except you didn't. You still harbor a quiet hope that there's a solution to developing a more expansive and diverse employee base, strengthening your corporate culture, and becoming more effective at reaching customers. This book is written for you because you have an important contribution to make. It's also written for the leader whose organization has real energy around a multiethnic workplace and a will to do something — but you don't know where to start.

Perhaps you're tired of the endless media debates on race in America and the political agendas tied to this complex topic. Perhaps you aren't entirely convinced all this fuss about race and ethnicity is worth it, but you're willing to have an open mind and see if this could really move your organization forward. I'll show you that building a multiethnic team creates more opportunities than inconveniences.

It's About Leadership

Let me tell you more about why I decided to write this book. Allow me to explain where I come from, what shaped my perspective, and why I'm versed in this topic. Well, it started in childhood. I grew up in the suburbs of four major cities: Chicago, Philadelphia, Washington, D.C., and New York. At an early age, I attended a racially diverse elementary school where over 30% of my classmates were African American. In my secondary education years, the schools I attended and the street I lived on were very multiethnic. Italian, Irish, Jewish, African American, Jamaican, and Hispanic people were all part of my community. Overnights at my friends' homes exposed me to cultures that were quite different from mine. This was the world I knew and was comfortable in—a world of various dialects, accents, and skin tones. It was a rich mixture of ethnicities and cultures.

In college, I developed a new group of diverse friends. When I decided to change schools, an incident occurred that served as a wake-up call that not everyone has the same comfort level with multiethnicity. Some of my white friends threw a party for me a couple of weeks before I left to attend another university. My white friends were first to arrive, but when my African American friends showed up, the atmosphere shifted. I was surprised when my white friends grew uncomfortable. To me, we had simply included my entire friend group, but my white friends didn't see it that way and eventually left in favor of a more homogenous environment.

While in my 20s, I met my wife—the joy of my life! As mentioned, she is African American, and we have three biological children together. The experiences we've had together have only enriched our lives and provided greater insight into the topics of race and ethnicity.

Lynne has also been my biggest cheerleader along my career journey, during which I spent several years leading cross-cultural teams at a global Fortune 1000 company. Over the years, I have held many leadership positions and have since become the co-founder of Transformational Executive Coaching, a consulting-training business that intentionally brings people together from diverse ethnic and racial backgrounds across for-profit and non-profit sectors, with the intent of developing better executives and transformational leaders. This two-year program helps leaders build more resilient, creative, and productive teams. Additionally, I've been active in supporting the work of two highly multiethnic churches.

Throughout my life, I've had the opportunity to engage in hundreds of local and global conversations on race and ethnicity. I even spent time in South Africa, where I listened to first-hand accounts of the horrors experienced by Apartheid. The after-effects of this diabolical system continue to plague that part of the world. Likewise, in the United States, we suffer from after-effects of racial segregation that greatly impact the racial and ethnic makeup of organizations.

So, my experience ranges from for-profit to non-profit, from business to church. I can assure you the principles outlined in this book apply to any type of organization. That's because real change is ultimately about leadership. As you'll see, this isn't a book about starting yet another well-intentioned but doomed-to-fail initiative. It's about encouraging and equipping leaders to take real steps toward progress.

Worth It

Are you wondering whether you can truly make a difference? When it comes to cultivating racial and ethnic diversity within an organization, self-doubt is not an uncommon reaction. And if we're keeping it real, it's not always an easy road. It can feel like an uphill battle against organizational resources and other stakeholders. Is it worth the hassle? We have a lot on our plates. With all the run-the-business activities going on, why take on this challenge?

Over the years, I've asked myself these same questions. Can I really affect change? Do I have the energy for this?

Is it worth the heartache and misunderstanding that often accompanies this conversation?

After years of both failed and successful attempts in different organizational contexts, it's clear to me that it's absolutely worthwhile. And a necessary reality given the continuing demographic shift in our country. The benefit to your organization and culture will be far greater than the challenge. Not only is it possible to create multiethnic teams and organizations, but it's also possible to create thriving, energized multiethnic organizations that are *winning in what they do*. The positive impact on your culture and on the lives of your team truly can't be quantified.

Reading This Book

To move forward, we need to consider the following: What can organizations do to make progress in becoming multiethnic? Practically speaking, what can leaders do to cultivate a thriving multiethnic organization?

While completing my Doctorate of Transformational Leadership with an emphasis on Entrepreneurial Organizational Transformation, the core of my research was focused on answering these questions. In this book, I want to boil down what I've discovered into the most essential takeaways for you, the busy leader.

One point of clarity: People often use the terms *racial diversity* and *multiethnic diversity* interchangeably, but they mean different things. *Race* is a cultural term used to categorize people based on physical traits regarded as common among people of shared ancestry. *Ethnicity* is a sociological term encompassing national, linguistic, and cultural origins as well as race. I use the term *multiethnic* because it's broader than racial diversity. It's inclusive of all ethnicities regardless of what part of the world your ancestors come from.

However, you will notice that most of the examples I share are about race. I want to highlight the fact that one of the main reasons we have such great divisions among people is because of our history of categorizing people according to skin color. In general, even among different ethnic groups, people who have felt the greatest discrimination have been people with darker skin complexion. (I recognize there are exceptions to this, like the discrimination felt by Jewish people.) Italian, Irish, and Polish people have faced some form of discrimination but not nearly as much as African American, Hispanic, Middle Eastern, and Asian Americans. For this reason, I sometimes use the terms *racial diversity* or *people of color* because these terms appropriately draw attention to this historical reality.

I do want to highlight, however, that the ideas espoused in this book apply to all ethnicities. Input was provided by several individuals from various countries, and each one acknowledged how applicable this is in their cultural context, so the application is broad and global.

This book is designed to be concise and highly practical. I don't intend to get into all the nuances of this complex topic. There are many other resources that delve into the multi-faceted aspects of race and ethnicity, and I encourage you to supplement this reading by seeking those out. There are other sources that go into great detail on the tools I discuss, such as interviews. Read whatever helps you move forward in becoming a healthier organization. This book is intended to provide practical first steps that help you begin your journey, gain real traction, and cultivate a thriving multiethnic organization.

While this book is designed to be a short read, *don't mistake its brevity for lack of depth*. This is an important topic that can challenge long-held assumptions and behaviors. Give yourself time to reflect and process ideas that may elicit resistance within you. You'll find it helpful to re-read some of the sections as you think more deeply about this subject. If you implement these ideas well, it will make a profound impact on you, your organization, and the communities you serve. Let this book inspire you to take action to begin and sustain new ways of growing yourself and your organization. So, please join me on the journey to elevating our organizations through racial and ethnic diversity!

My research included hours and hours of interviews with high-level leaders from the for-profit and nonprofit sectors. I've conducted focus groups and trainings with all organizational levels. In summary, I identified four themes or spheres of influence that leaders should actively pursue to successfully implement a multiethnic workplace:

1. **Vision and Ownership**: Top leader buy-in, ownership, and accountability

2. **Process Reset**: Revitalized attraction, selection, and retention processes

3. **Employee Engagement**: Ongoing training and dialogue for every employee

4. **Inspiration and Guidance**: Use of a coach, guiding team, and debriefing

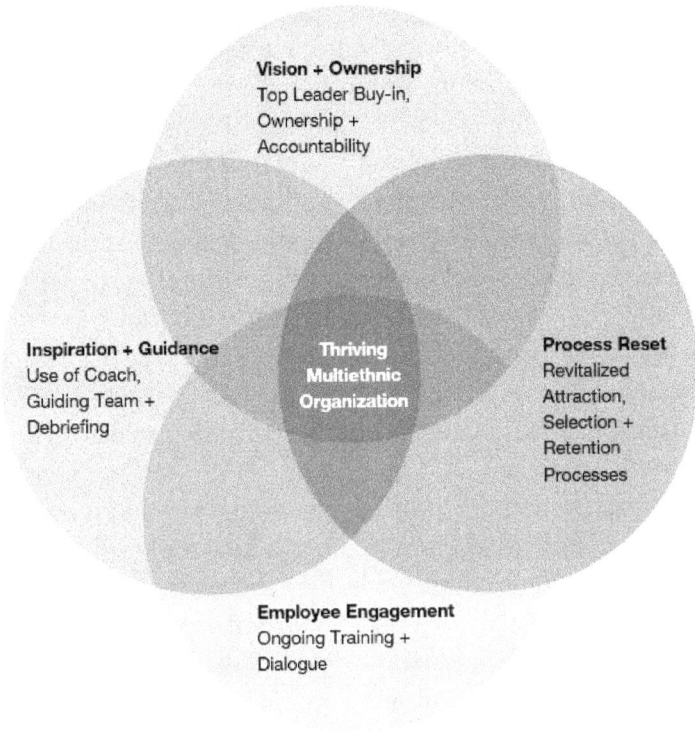

Vision + Ownership
Top Leader Buy-in,
Ownership +
Accountability

Inspiration + Guidance
Use of Coach,
Guiding Team +
Debriefing

**Thriving
Multiethnic
Organization**

Process Reset
Revitalized
Attraction,
Selection +
Retention
Processes

Employee Engagement
Ongoing Training +
Dialogue

Thriving multiethnic organizations succeed in large part by addressing all four spheres. They take a holistic and process-oriented approach.

Organizations moving into this territory should feel encouraged by the fact that others have been where you are now. These organizations didn't start out as multiethnic workplaces. They had to learn how to become one. That means there's a process you can apply in your organization. I can't promise it will be easy. But I can promise that it will be rewarding and highly beneficial. If you're in an especially entrenched institution, trying to influence a culture change can make your life miserable. But we don't create multiethnic organizations because it's the easy thing to do; we do it because it makes our organizations and communities better.

Some organizations might not see the point in embracing multiethnicity when the communities where they reside have very little ethnic diversity. I get it. It may be true that, at best, you will only attract a few ethnically diverse people to your organization. Learning to do this well with the few that you have, however, makes your organization that much better now and in years to come. It creates a better experience for those who enter your organization and prepares you for any demographic change that takes place in the future. Yes, you create an *advantage* for your organization when cultivating multiethnicity!

In the remaining pages, we're going to look at each of the identified four themes to unpack how they will help you execute your multiethnic goals. First, however, we need to get on the same page about a very important aspect of this whole conversation: Why we're doing this at all.

CAVEAT: As mentioned, opinions vary widely on this topic. Some will differ regarding certain points I make or wish I highlighted other ethnic groups and their plight. This book is not intended to be all-encompassing, and I will be the first to say I'm open to new perspectives and am a life-long learner on this subject. Nevertheless, I'm sharing my thoughts and insights based on my lived experience, and I believe there are some very important ideas that will benefit you and your organization whether you resonate with everything I say or not.

CHAPTER ONE

Why?

When you know your why, you can endure any how.
—Victor Frankl

One shining example of a multiethnic organization is Trinity Health Grand Rapids (formerly Mercy Health Saint Mary's). For years, they were focused on increasing racial diversity. Yet, the Grand Rapids location continued to remain slightly below the community average. During this time, the chief human resources officer (CHRO) envisioned a hiring process that would minimize bias and stereotypes and, at the end of the day, put the right people in the right jobs. The result? Over a five-year period, they doubled their racial diversity percentage![10]

At first glance, it looks like this change is largely due to a process change, and it's true that the process change was key (more on that in Chapter Three). However, this great transformation happened because the CHRO articulated his WHY. He had a vision, laid out the case to the organization's stakeholders, and got real buy-in that allowed them to enact change.

Simon Sinek, author of *Start With WHY*, popularized the idea of finding our core reason for doing what we do.[11] Sinek is famous for his golden circle diagram, which helps us understand the source of our motivation—our WHY. As leaders, we must examine this closely. WHY should an organization pursue a multiethnic initiative? WHY should an organization look to become racially diverse? These are key questions we must answer.

The hard work of organizational transformation requires a vision to give it momentum and keep it on course when obstacles threaten to stop progress. The people pushing and pulling to create the transformation need to have more than good intentions or a mandate or even a budget line. You need a captivating vision of what you're trying to create and why you're doing it, and that vision needs to run through the organization from top to bottom.

The Business Case

Maybe you have your vision and are committed, but is this simply the right thing to do—or the right thing for the company's bottom line? Personally, I believe the moral case for multiethnicity is preeminent, but I know that questions of cost and the bottom line are also important. Compellingly, there are several well-founded business reasons for moving in a multiethnic direction.

For one, your talent pool is greatly enhanced as you tap into new recruiting pipelines. Having good labor is key to an organization's success and is especially pertinent given today's labor challenges. Sometimes, leaders have an unexamined belief that there aren't viable candidates outside their current majority white talent pool. The reverse is actually the case. People of color, and women, for that matter, will tell you they've had to work extra hard and become highly resilient to achieve what they have. Did you know that having a strong work ethic is often one of the main cultural characteristics of people of color?[12] In pursuing multiethnicity, you will often add people with strong work ethics, high achievement standards, and incredible skills to your talent pool. Why not attract and retain the best and brightest?

Additionally, having greater racial and ethnic diversity can lead to greater diversity of thought, which in turn leads to better ideas, creativity, and innovation. Stronger and healthier cultures are often created when people from diverse backgrounds come together in the workplace. We often say we don't want to surround ourselves with "yes people." In reality, it's very easy to do just that if we're not being intentional.

Building a multiethnic team is a powerful tool for helping you and your team break out of unconscious habits of thought that could be keeping your business in a rut. Frankly, many organizations are global, and the ability to facilitate work across cultures is critical to success. Doing this well is dependent on trust and collaboration across cultures.

In a global company I worked for, there often was a reluctance on the part of Americans to share work with team members in other countries. Some people were more culturally open, but many were not. I recently discussed this topic with a former colleague who lives in another country and is part of a global team. This person confided that although it's better than fifteen years ago, she still senses a reluctance at times, hindering the progress of effectively sharing work. Successful global teams understand the value of multiethnic diversity and willingly work through all of its challenges.

There is also some evidence that suggests multiethnicity is good for the bottom line. A McKinsey report on 366 public companies found that those in the top quartile for ethnic and racial diversity in management were 35% more likely to have financial returns above their industry mean.[13] The report concluded that diverse teams are smarter.

Research suggests that diverse teams have greater cultural sensitivity, insight, and market knowledge, which can make a business more competitive and profitable. As mentioned, diverse cultural perspectives can inspire creativity and drive innovation. Diverse teams can be more productive and perform better, and they provide a great opportunity for personal and professional growth. The bottom line is when you look to expand your employee base, you're making an investment that bolsters your human capital.

Cost?

Someone will undoubtedly ask, "But what about the cost to implement?" Fred Keller (owner and founder of a successful global business, Cascade Engineering) responded to this question by commenting, "We have upside-down thinking about all of this. In business, we look at the ROI, and then we prioritize. We never get down to the social opportunities because the ROI is low, and we don't know how to measure them…but they don't cost much either." Hear what he's saying? Prioritize it—even if we can't find clear measures. It's the right thing to do, and in the end, it *will cost you very little.*

Business Is Human

While there's evidence to support that multiethnicity is good for the bottom line, it's also important to acknowledge another aspect. Human beings are moral creatures, and business, or any type of work for that matter is a human activity. It doesn't do us any good to pretend it's not. When people are treated well, we do better business. This is why improving your employee engagement, deepening employees' sense of satisfaction at work, etc., is often measured and evaluated.

Books like Dennis Bakke's *Joy At Work*, Joel Manby's *Love Works*, Brene Brown's *Dare to Lead*, and Richard Sheridan's *Chief Joy Officer* often resonate with business leaders. These books speak to the human side of work. In fact, when leaders create a successful business, they often turn their attention towards the social impact they can make in their place of work and in their local communities. They recognize the opportunity to impact people's lives and understand that if they create an environment that allows all people to flourish—to really enjoy coming to work—they are impacting people in positive ways that go well beyond the bottom line. Business suddenly has a purpose beyond making profits; it's a social good. The positive energy and passion that comes from being treated well carries people through all kinds of challenges in life.

So, yes, cultivating a healthy multiethnic organization is an investment in people that often leads to better returns, a superior talent pool, and a more engaged workforce. But there are good moral reasons to pursue multiethnicity as well.

The Moral Case

In an article entitled, "Walking the Talk on Diversity: CEO Beliefs, Moral Values and the Implementation of Workplace Diversity Practices," Eddy Ng and Greg Sears suggest that leaders should argue diversity is the "right thing to do" even if it doesn't bear a financial return.[14] They say that "one's moral values are critical for framing diversity initiatives when the business case for diversity is weak." In other words, appealing to people's sense of morality might be a better way to gain support for multiethnic diversity in your organization when they are skeptical about the business case.

I can get on board with that train of thought. We can take the business case seriously, but we should highlight the moral one. Appealing to people's sense of fairness often strikes the right chord in preparing an organization for multiethnic change. It's about creating a team that looks more like our community and country and creates equal opportunity for everyone. It's about recognizing the real skills and value that people of all ethnicities have to offer.

A moral justification is often more effective in gaining the desired support. As Fred Keller told me regarding this subject,

"Use the 'right thing' as your north star... It's a tremendous corporate social opportunity... Why would we not do it?"

Yes, there's work involved in getting it off the ground, but it's what's best for everyone and comes with little cost. In addition, this isn't an either-or situation. Although I emphasize the moral case, you will benefit from the business case. Ultimately, it's a win-win. It's good for people and good for business, and there's a great return waiting for those who pursue this path.

The beauty of multiethnicity in the workplace is that it builds relationships among people who've been divided historically. As relationships form, empathy grows. As empathy grows, biases are brought to the surface and often corrected. As biases are corrected, racial and ethnic healing takes place. This happens best in personal relationships as one colleague gets to know another. This may seem far-fetched, but don't discount what can happen when people connect in the workplace. In truth, your organization promotes a lot of things you may be unaware of. Why wouldn't you want it to be a place where you promote positive relationships among people who are ethnically different?

The Author's WHY

As I previously mentioned, I'm a white male who grew up in the suburbs of four large cities. I was raised in a middle-class home, but unlike most people who grew up in this environment, I had an abundance of multiethnic experiences that shaped my life.

As a six or seven-year-old boy, I saw a white classmate throw stones at an African American kid, calling him the N-word while outside a museum in the city of Chicago. I intuitively knew this was wrong and done solely because of his skin color. Experiences like this can teach a kid who witnesses this behavior to hate others because of their skin color, or it can have the opposite effect as it did with me.

When I moved to a New York City suburb one month after my eighth-grade school year began, it was a group of African American guys who were the first to welcome me. And when I went into the lunchroom not knowing a soul, this same group asked me to join them at their lunch table. I was immediately accepted and welcomed. The truth was, at times, I felt more accepted for who I was with my African American friends than my white peers. There was an authenticity and acceptance I experienced that allowed me to be receptive and open to multiethnic relationships.

The street I lived on in White Plains, New York, housed a diverse group of ethnicities, including an African American family. I became great friends with two members of this family. Prior to moving into the neighborhood, their house caught fire and burned down. The fire was clearly caused by arson. Someone didn't want a black family to move into our neighborhood. To their credit, this strong family patiently waited to have their house rebuilt and moved into it anyway. Can you imagine having to decide if you wanted to move into a neighborhood where someone burned your house down because they didn't like your skin color?

My neighborhood friends had to put up with insensitive comments about race from one of our neighbors. The father of another neighbor told his kids not to let my friends set foot on their property because they were black. I was called an N-lover by a white bully at our school's bus stop. These experiences caused me more and more to question why these things happened. Why would someone in our neighborhood want this family's house burned down? What is it about a person's skin color that engenders these feelings? Why would this white guy call me a racist name at the bus stop when my black friend wasn't there? Why do all of these things happen simply because of a person's skin color?

As I reflected on my experiences, the impact of race became more and more apparent. And for all the whites I knew, it just didn't matter. They were busy with their lives, doing their thing, and accepting of the status quo. Sure, they might be sympathetic to what people of color experience, but if it didn't impact them, there was no cause for action or reason to change. After all, what could they really do?

As I grew into my late teens, I began to wonder even more. Why are people who are the same as whites (biologically, emotionally, intellectually...) often stereotyped in such a way that they're excluded from some of the better things in life, like housing, education, and jobs? Keep in mind: I'm speaking in general terms. I recognize that not all people of color have been treated poorly, and many enjoy the finer things in life. However, as a kid growing up, these were my observations.

When I entered the workplace, I noticed the professional ranks had very few people of color. Yet, in the factory and manual labor jobs, there was a high concentration. Why was this? I attempted several times to help organizations I worked for become more racially diverse. This required a lot of energy and effort. Most of the people I engaged with appreciated the idea, but it wasn't compelling enough to become a priority with staying power. Why wasn't it a priority?

It's something that's challenged and troubled me on some level for most of my life. I've always known that something wasn't right. Why are black people treated differently from whites? Why are the jokes typically about every ethnic group except whites? Why is there such a lack of people of color in the professional ranks? How do we start thinking outside of this box that holds people back? This caused me to wonder: How can we make progress, and how can I make a difference? What's one place we can focus on to really make an impact?

I write this book to explain why this matters and how to move forward. Some will say that all of our racial problems are in the past, and we've come a long way since then. I acknowledge that much progress has been made over the years. However, the reality is that racial equity is still an important issue needing attention. There's still a huge gap in the professional ranks when it comes to hiring people of color. When I'm in a room discussing organizational tactics and strategies, I know we're better if we're a diverse group of people. The more we include all people—all ethnicities—the more we win as an organization and a society.

There are many leaders today who like the idea of growing more racially and ethnically diverse but don't know how to do it. Some leaders don't like what's being promoted in certain diversity circles, so they'd prefer to avoid it. It seems too controversial, so why go there? Others feel alienated when trying to have a conversation around this topic, so why put yourself out there? I've wrestled with these questions, too. I understand the concern, but if you look at what I propose, I believe you'll find a fresh and positive way forward.

Over the years, it's become clear to me that most of us don't realize how much of our thinking on race and ethnicity has been shaped by our country's past, our parents' and grandparents' views on race, the schools we attended, the people we hung out with, hidden race-related policies and practices, and the media's portrayal of this issue. Frankly, most of us don't realize the racial bias we possess that unknowingly nudges us away from multiethnicity in favor of the familiar.

Larger Impact

One other thing to consider: Think of all the people who've been harmed, demeaned, or marginalized in some way because of the prejudice and racism that's marked this country since its inception—whether you use 1492, 1619[15], or 1776 as the key date. Our country's history has an ugly side to it, and people today carry with them the inherited social and economic legacy of that history. If you ignore what's taken place and its lingering effects, you'll miss out on an opportunity to benefit all human beings.[16] In the long run, ethnic diversity will not only make your organization and community better, but it's not too grandiose to say it will improve our humanity and us as a nation. One relationship at a time.

I've always had a passion to connect people, to build bridges. This might be in part due to my multiethnic experiences over the years, but regardless, bridge-building is inherent within me. My faith informs me that all people are made in the image of God, and it's my responsibility to steward and cultivate this world for the better. In whatever sphere of influence I have, I want our world to be better when I leave it. I want to help leaders get past the externals, get past all the chatter and tension on this topic, and discern the heart of the matter. I want you to see how much better we all can be if we have a vision, develop a plan, and pursue a path toward a multiethnic organization. Yes, there is an *advantage* in a multiethnic organization!

CHAPTER TWO

Vision and Ownership

Where there is no vision, the people perish.
—Proverbs 29:18 (KJV)

**Vision +
Ownership**
Top Leader Buy-in,
Ownership +
Accountability

n my research interviews, I asked, "Which local organizations are doing multiethnic diversity well?" I posed this question to high-level leaders representing all manner of organizations. Can you guess the most common answer? *Nobody.* That's depressing, to say the least, but we mustn't be discouraged. To begin with, it's not entirely accurate. Rather, it tells us how little awareness there is of these initiatives. In addition, it tells us that even organizations making great strides feel inadequate and recognize there's still room to grow.

However, several leaders named Cascade Engineering and Trinity Health Grand Rapids as organizations that cultivated meaningful change. People familiar with their stories affirmed that these organizations were transformed because the top leaders made it a priority to stay the course. Are they perfect in how they handle multiethnicity? No. Employees from these organizations would say they still have room for improvement. However, these organizations made great headway because leadership made it a priority and didn't give up when facing difficulties.

Fred Keller told me that on his company's (Cascade Engineering) journey to become racially diverse, there were several setbacks along the way. He could have concluded, as many people do, that it isn't possible or isn't worth it or that it was enough just to try. Instead, he held on to his vision, which was to build a business where people loved coming to work. He wanted the workplace to be a place where everyone—regardless of ethnicity—felt valued. He made it clear to his leaders that failure was part of the process. The key was learning from it. Instead of giving up, they kept trying different approaches until there was progress. Today, this organization has become a model for others.

Top Leader Ownership

> *Leaders must own everything in their world.*
> *There is no one else to blame.*
> —Jocko Willink

When I interviewed with the company president for my current role, I told him about my doctoral research. I asked if he had an interest in helping implement some of my recommendations. To my surprise, he was very supportive. I couldn't believe it! At best, I expected a mediocre response, knowing every organization has a lot on its plate. Yet, he was willing to make cultivating a multiethnic organization a priority despite all the other things clamoring for his attention.

If you've ever tried to do this work, then you understand this is rare and special. Years ago, I attempted to get a racial diversity initiative off the ground in a Fortune 1000 company. I was in sales and worked with human resources to create a program that partnered with local high schools to bring minority students to our company and expose them to various career opportunities. My hope was that students would build relationships with company leaders to spawn an interest in working for our company. The program lasted for several years. Eventually, I moved on to another position and had a good friend take the lead on orchestrating the program.

A couple of years later, my friend left the company...and the program died. Why? No one at the higher levels made it a priority. It was viewed as "nice-to-have" but not of great importance. The program survived only as long as someone led the charge and gave energy to it.

In every organization I've been part of, I've attempted in some way to help them become more multiethnic. All of these organizations were receptive to the idea (which was great), but not all made progress. They acknowledged they could get better but weren't all willing to sign up for a serious commitment. This is why top leader buy-in is the critical piece in moving an organization forward in a multiethnic direction.

Every leader I interviewed agreed that the biggest obstacle in cultivating a multiethnic organization is leader buy-in at the highest levels. Leaders need to have a heart for this type of change because the road is long and challenging. One HR leader told me her organization had great success in becoming racially diverse because the previous two presidents of the organization were servant leaders. They had a servant's heart, really cared about the issue, and were willing to do what was needed. They wanted to make a difference and were unwilling to let obstacles derail them. If the leader doesn't have a strong desire to take the organization in a multiethnic direction, it won't happen. Period! Top-level leaders must have a sincere interest in this topic, or it won't have staying power. Any real progress in cultivating a multiethnic organization must start and be prioritized at the top.

Once this piece is in place, there must be an overarching desire to keep it as a priority. I'll never forget the time when a company I worked for decided to promote a new operations initiative. We were going to stop a problem that arose every summer when vacations were high, and customer orders increased. Top leaders were behind it, and department heads were serious about making the improvements needed. As one of the leaders, I was very supportive of the idea. Yet, despite the desire to address the problem, we weren't successful.

What happened? After the initiative was launched, other issues cropped up that stole our attention. The initiative eventually lost steam, and we didn't accomplish what we had set out to do. It's one thing to make it a priority when you get something started, but if you don't keep it in the spotlight, it will be lost in the shuffle of other initiatives.

Over the years, I've seen this pattern repeated often with the best-intentioned initiatives. The highest-level leaders were genuine in what they wanted to accomplish. In a number of cases, I was personally involved with the implementation. Yet, these initiatives quickly lost traction as we got caught up in the daily problems we were trying to solve. So, what do we do?

Franklin-Covey developed a concept called "wildly important goals" (WIGs), defined as key critical objectives that must be achieved regardless of the climate.[17] The tendency for most of us is to take on too many goals. This waters down our ability to accomplish what matters most. In their research (published in *The 4 Disciplines of Execution*), Franklin-Covey found if organizations want to accomplish a goal of critical importance, they must focus on only one or two. This doesn't mean there aren't other initiatives an organization pursues. It does mean, however, that if it's deemed a critical goal, leaders must clear the deck to ensure it gets proper attention. For this reason, cultivating a healthy multiethnic organization must be prioritized in such a way that the urgencies of the day don't diminish it.

Simply put, if top leaders do not keep cultivating a multiethnic organization as a priority, it will quickly lose steam and be left in the wake of run-the-business matters. Top-level leader buy-in and ownership are critical to the success of any multiethnic initiative.

Messaging

When the decision is made to create a multiethnic organization, the leaders must be sensitive and thoughtful about their messaging around this change. It's crucial to create clarity about the importance of the desired change. First, it needs to be communicated to everyone in leadership so there's support and energy behind it. Secondly, the topic of racial diversity must be handled sensitively. After the leadership is on board, gaining the mindshare and support of an organization's members is the next important step. Handling this topic in a way that helps people understand why you're doing it and having the full support of management goes a long way toward gaining employee support and buy-in.

Transparency is a virtue in this work; it helps build trust and provides resilience when things don't go as planned. As an example, in an effort to bring change to my current organization (Lumbermen's), we decided to ground the initiative in our company values and promote it as an expression of them. We made it clear that we're choosing the topic of racial diversity because it's been a problem in the United States since its foundation, and we want to be part of the solution. This is a complex problem with no quick fix, but we want people to understand that *we can* make a difference in our organization.

Engaging employees in conversation that raises their awareness and understanding of this issue helps encourage a culture of racial and ethnic inclusivity. In essence, you're communicating that it's the right thing to do and will positively impact your organization and community. By broadcasting this up front, we're inviting our employees into our WHY so they can be part of the transformation.

One important point: If handled well, this topic can be a healthy conversation. Not that it won't have its detractors, but the approach I'm suggesting is designed to minimize fall out and negativity and encourage more of a positive tone within your organization.

Make a Plan

> By failing to prepare, you are preparing to fail.
> —Benjamin Franklin

"How do we get there?" This is the question people ask when pursuing transformational change. If top-level leaders agree in principle on the importance of cultivating a multiethnic organization, the next step is creating a plan for implementation.

For any initiative to gain serious traction, there must be a well-developed plan. A change management plan helps ensure forward movement in the effort to become multi-ethnic. As Linda Ackerman-Anderson and Dean Anderson state in *The Change Leader's Roadmap*, "The most prevalent type of change in organizations today is transformation... Leaders must create the capabilities, infrastructures, mindsets, and behaviors they require. Both leaders and consultants must learn how to masterfully guide transformational change."[18]

The challenge, as change guru John Kotter explains in *Leading Change*, is that organizations often overestimate how much change they can implement and underestimate how hard it is to enact.[19] The Anderson's add in *Beyond Change Management*, "Another part of the issue is poor change leadership, which gives change a bad name in the minds of the employees. Most leaders design and execute lousy change processes, and when the process of change is bad, the experience of change is bad."[20]

Underestimating what's involved in the change process will lead to poor results and bad attitudes surrounding the change. Change is tricky and must be navigated carefully in order to avoid obstacles that threaten progress.

In *HBR's 10 Must Reads on Change Management*, Garvin and Roberto identify six tendencies that stop change in it its tracks.[21] Significantly, these include:

- Having a culture of "no."

- Allowing politics to derail the initiative.

- Not having a definitive course of action.

Without a plan, cultivating multiethnicity will never be more than a perennial talking point.

Most of the change initiatives I've participated in have fallen far short of their goals. Of the few that were successful, all of them *addressed key steps in the change process* and *developed a system of accountability* to ensure follow-through of the plan. In short, the ones that were successful had a plan that was consistently followed.

One time, at the Fortune 1000 company I worked for, we decided to change our customer service model from an individual service approach to one that was team-based. The one thing that allowed us to stay the course was having a change management plan based upon John Kotter's 8-Steps For Leading Change.[22] Having regular leadership meetings that covered each of these steps helped us stay the course and implement the initiative successfully. I can't tell you how many obstacles emerged that would have derailed the whole thing if we hadn't had a plan and followed it—you have probably experienced many of them yourself. We would've gone backward if we didn't stick to the roadmap. Whether it's multiethnicity or any significant change, having a solid plan is crucial.

Transformation

> *Transformation isn't a future event.*
> *It's a present-day activity.*
> —Jillian Michaels

The term *transformation* is used loosely these days to indicate any type of change that takes place. It helps us feel better about how little progress we're making to say that such-and-such "transformed" the company when we know all it really did was make it easier to re-order office supplies. Real transformation is difficult, comprehensive, and long-lasting. In *Leadership from the Inside Out*, Kevin Cashman says, "Transformation is not an event but a challenging process of working through the coaching needs of leaders, teams, and organizations simultaneously."[23] Transformational leadership is a holistic approach to leadership. It's a long-term process engaging everyone in the organization that eventually leads to sustainable change.

Real transformation requires intentional focus and staying the course over the long haul. Lasting change doesn't happen overnight; it happens incrementally over a long period of time. Whether it's Michael Jordan or Warren Buffet, you become highly successful because of a daily, sustained effort over time—often many years. Sports teams that have a long stretch of success don't begin with many years of successful playoff runs. L.L. Bean didn't start as a company with decades of success behind it. These organizations succeed because of a daily, sustained regimen of implementing ideas and refining them into best practices.

In other words, transformation occurs when top leadership is committed to a long, slow walk rather than a short sprint. If multiethnic diversity is important, it must be prioritized as a key initiative that is sustained over the long haul. If not, any progress will be short-lived and go the way of the dreaded "program of the month." These initiatives get tossed aside as soon as another priority captures the mind of the leader.

Pain and Fear

> *If we do not transform our pain,*
> *we will most assuredly transmit it.*
> —Richard Rohr

There's another aspect of transformation that's unique to the multiethnic journey. Reflect on the quote above. "If we do not transform our pain, we will most assuredly transmit it." There are many painful stories when it comes to race in America. Although progress has been made, racism and its effects run deep. If we don't venture down the multiethnic path, this disregarded pain will continue to derail us and literally be transmitted to future generations. How many of us have acquired ideas espoused by our parents? How many of us have unknowingly taken on attitudes and dispositions towards those who are ethnically different without ever thinking about where they come from?

People of color often carry generations of pain with them. Let me be clear: it's not part of this initiative to presume anyone has such pain or to take on the role of therapy, but it's important, on the one hand, to be aware that this pain may surface in unexpected ways and, on the other hand, to recognize that multiethnic work is part of healing that pain.

Michael Poutiatine states that transformation "always involves some aspect of risk, fear, and loss…[it] involves a broadening of the scope of worldview."[24] This is exactly what must take place to cultivate a thriving multiethnic organization, but you can see why it's difficult. When people see their familiar order apparently under threat, they often get protective, withdrawn, fearful, and angry. In order to navigate these challenges, we need to look closely at key factors that drive an organization toward positive multiethnic transformation.

Singular Focus

> *I focus on one thing and one thing only.*
> —Kobe Bryant

Most organizations look to capture racial diversity under the broader umbrella of diversity, thinking that all boats rise together. You might be surprised to learn that, in my experience, racial diversity gains little traction because it often gets buried among other diversity initiatives. Resources are limited, so it's easy to get lost in the shuffle as other forms of diversity get attention or may be easier to pursue. Most people don't realize that evidence suggests that affirmative action disproportionately benefited white women more than people of color.[25] When racial diversity is mixed in with other forms of diversity, it often fades into the background. True racial and ethnic equality is not easy to obtain, so if we're not singularly focused on multiethnic diversity, we won't get the results we're looking for.

We must also remember that race has been a major problem in our country for several hundred years. African Americans are the one group of people who came to this country against their will. Native Americans have another important story to tell, including being forcibly removed from their homes under Andrew Jackson's Indian Removal Act.[26] All other people groups (German, English, Mexican, Italian, Japanese…) came seeking a better life. The net out is that our country enforced practices for years that negatively impacted those with darker skin color, and we're still dealing with the after-effects. Let me be clear. I'm not saying great gains haven't been made—they have. However, it's important to understand how our history has impacted economic and social systems (housing, education, hiring…), which have lingering effects today.

Historically, we must recognize that preferential treatment has generally been given to people with lighter skin tones. Think of how long it took whites to accept the idea of a black quarterback or a black head coach in the NFL. This wasn't that long ago. Spike Lee's *School Daze* dramatizes the impact internalized racism has had within the black community by putting light-skinned and dark-skinned black people in conflict. *Racial* and ethnic diversity continues to be a challenge for our country. This is why it's important to highlight this topic as a singular initiative. Focusing on it this way gives it the full attention needed to make progress and inspire real change.

5 Takeaways from Implementing Change Plans

Any multiethnic change plan will be complex, multifaceted, and difficult to implement. I have had success with Kotter's 8-Steps, but I have also seen success with other strategies, including *ad hoc* ones created in the meeting room. Rather than recommending this or that model, I'd like to share five key takeaways I've learned from working on change plans. No matter which you use, keep these five principles in mind.

1 – Understand the Change Curve.

The Change Curve is a popular model that is used to understand the stages of personal transition and organizational change.[27] In the workplace, the change curve can help predict how employees will react to change. By understanding the change curve, you can successfully guide your team through changes, making their transition as manageable as possible. I used a version of this with one of my leadership teams to prepare them for a major organizational structure change that impacted over 80 people. It was also shared with employees when the change was first announced to help them understand how this change might affect them.

The purpose of this model is to provide perspective on what happens when you implement change. For instance, it's quite normal for productivity to decline when a change is first implemented. Discussing this beforehand prepares the organization for what lies ahead. With multiethnic change, there isn't so much of a productivity decline as a period of emotional adjustment. There's often some sort of emotional transition in how people feel at the very beginning of multiethnic change. One of the main reasons for this is that it's not a conversation that typically happens in the workplace, so people have to get more comfortable with having this type of dialogue.

According to this model, there are different phases people go through when experiencing change. The "denial" phase is where people deny that there's a need for change. They're focused on the uncomfortable nature of the conversation and believe it shouldn't be discussed at work. It's during this phase where relevant information is presented to help people understand why we're doing this. We then move into an "anger" phase, where people realize the change isn't going away and are upset over what's happening. Moreover, people are wrestling with their own biases and not liking how it makes them feel. In this stage, it's important to be empathetic (offer support) while reinforcing the purpose of the initiative.

After this phase, there's a movement towards the "exploration" phase, where people realize the change is here to stay, so they need to adapt to it. It's during this time that direction is provided to ensure the change sticks. Lastly, people move into the "acceptance" phase, where the need to change is accepted and understood. In this last phase, people have embraced and begun to lean into the change. During this segment, encouragement is offered to continue the positive momentum.

The Change Curve

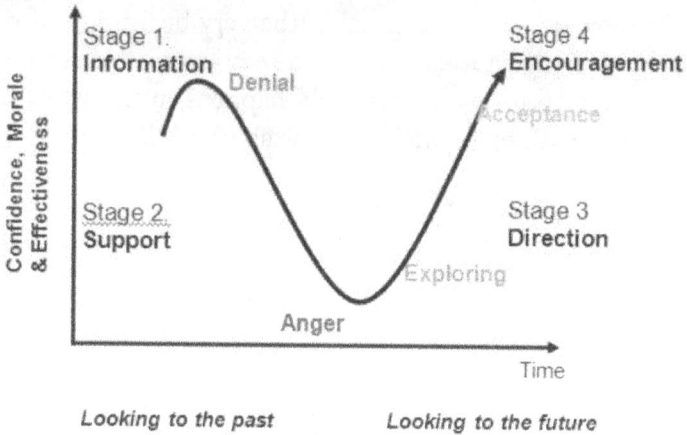

(https://www.educational-business-articles.com/
change-curve/#google_vignette)

As the model indicates, specific actions are needed in each phase to help people move forward. For example, in the denial or anger phase, it can be useful to have people name their fears. When it comes to moving towards multiethnicity, the fears might be:

- losing out on job opportunities
- moving away from a comfortable culture
- quotas will exist, and the best candidate won't be hired
- hiring practices will become biased toward race
- this initiative is tied to Critical Race Theory (CRT)[28] or some other ideology
- we'll be talking about issues that have no place in the workplace

These fears are real and must be spoken to in order to disarm them. As an example, I clarify at the outset that this initiative is not connected to CRT or any other ideology. I reiterate frequently that this isn't about racial quotas. I state emphatically that we always strive to hire the best person for the job. I then clarify that we're attempting to expand our recruiting pipeline so we have better talent to draw from. If the best person is a person of color or minority, we want to communicate that we're a good organization for them to join. This helps reinforce our sensitivity to the issue while alleviating the concern.

2 – Plan for the Mess.

According to Kotter's experience, well over 50% of companies fail in the first phase.[29] These organizations didn't adequately plan for change and, importantly, underestimated what it takes to make it stick. Skipping steps in the change process never produces satisfying results.

Most successful change efforts are messy and full of surprises. This must be understood throughout the process, or the initiative will likely lose steam and die.

3 – Anticipate the Temptation to Quit.

This point corresponds with point number two. When leaders embark on cultivating a multiethnic culture, they must remember that change is hard at first, messy in the middle, but very rewarding at the end. It's of critical importance to not let uncertainty deter you when you're in the middle of the change.

I'm not suggesting that you don't ever scrap or adjust a change initiative if you get clear signs it is misguided or has a flaw in the plan. Sometimes, ending a change is necessary, but this should be rare and framed as a learning experience. Abandoning a change plan should never be confused with abandoning your core values—your WHY. You will face unexpected obstacles. You will face uncertainty. Ask whether it's a good plan that needs tweaking or a bad plan that needs to go. Every change worth its salt will involve a messy period, so feeling uncertain should be perceived as entirely normal.

4 - Remember the 10-80-10 Rule.[30]

This rule states that, on average, 10% of the people in an organization will support the change, 80% will be somewhere in the middle, taking a "wait and see" approach, and 10% will be dead set against it. Leaders need to direct their attention to the 80% since this group can be swayed either way.

You'll always have detractors, so you'll want to be selective in how much time you spend with this group and not let their negativity derail you. Establish proper boundaries that allow you to hear their concerns with empathy without scrambling to please everyone. Instead, focus your attention on the 80% in order to move them to the supporter camp. Once this happens, the resistant 10% tend to come along.

5 – Never Forget That a Negative Attitude Will Kill Your Ability to Adapt to Change.

I've emphasized this to many leaders during the change process. I've also shared this with employees who are resistant to change. Our brains are wired in such a way that if we allow ourselves to become negative, it prevents us from adapting to change. This is important for everyone to understand as our mindset can change.[31] In most cases, the initiative is going to happen, so it's better not to fight the inevitable. We must help our teams keep the WHY in view and remind them that cultivating a positive attitude will help them adapt to the new order.

Getting Started

1. Develop your WHY and vision. Write them down.

2. Clarify the business and moral case.

3. Ensure your leaders are bought in and own the change.

4. Develop and own your change plan.

5. Remember the change curve. Prepare to support people during each phase of the change.

CHAPTER THREE

Process Reset

The biggest room in the world is the room for improvement.
—Helmut Schmidt

Vision + Ownership
Top Leader Buy-in,
Ownership +
Accountab

Process Reset
Revitalized
Attraction,
Selection +
Retention
Processes

Attraction, Selection, & Retention Processes

*Nothing we do is more important than hiring and
developing people. At the end of the day,
you bet on people, not on strategies.*
—Lawrence Bossidy

Everything is designed. Few things are designed well.
—Brian Reed

After top leaders decide to own, develop, and implement a plan, the next step is to assess and modify existing attraction, selection, and retention processes. Your current human resource systems are designed in ways that encourage certain results. The design of these systems must be looked at closely if you want to cultivate a more robust workforce.

As one leader shared, cultivating a multiethnic organization is more than a social imperative; it's a systemic priority. In other words, it's a design problem. In the United States, we've seen how the system of segregation throughout the last century created racial inequity and injustice that we're still dealing with today. In short, segregation was a horrible design that led to dreadful results.

If you're serious about cultivating positive multiethnic change, you must look at your organizational systems and discern how to make them better. In essence, you must rethink your design in order to bring about better results. All of your human resource systems (recruiting, interviewing, hiring, onboarding, mentoring, and advancement) need to be assessed. These processes must be fine-tuned to neutralize bias, ensure the organization is tapping into new recruiting pipelines, and create a welcoming environment for all. Let's look at a couple of these processes.

Recruiting Pipeline

> *Your human talent is your most important talent.*
> —Carla Harris

"We're hiring the best candidates, but people of color are not applying."

"We've hired some minorities in the factory but none in the office."

"It looks to me like the talent pool is just too limited."

These are common refrains from many leaders. They've tried to do the right thing by looking for multiethnic hires, but they can't hire people who aren't applying.

Every organization has its recruiting pipelines. This might be local colleges and universities, high schools, social media, online ads, or staffing agencies. And it's true that many of those pipelines are largely filled with white candidates, but it's like fishing in the same spot. You might want to attract different types of fish, but if they don't frequent where you're fishing, you'll never catch them. Expanding your recruiting pipeline is necessary for gaining traction in this area. This may sound simple, but it will require focus and persistence, or it won't happen.

The one recruiting pipeline often overlooked by organizations is their own people. A high percentage of new hires come from employee references. In fact, this is often the reason people enter the organization—because they know someone there. In many ways, this is the best method for bringing in new talent. But if the employee base is monoracial or monocultural, you'll continue to bring in the same type of people. We tend to hire people we resonate with and who happen to be part of our personal network. They tend to all share important similarities with us, and if we're white, these people are likely white. Stepping out of your comfort zone to expand your network isn't always easy, but it's necessary if you want to see change.

Likewise, as you diversify the people entering the organization, there's an opportunity to build on the diversity that's occurred. Encouraging people of color in your organization to reach out to their friends and relatives is a great way to increase multiethnic diversity. At the very least, it will help create a more diverse candidate pool.

Additionally, there are many networks in your local community that can help expand your recruiting pipeline. These networks will gladly promote your organization's job opportunities to people you normally wouldn't reach. The local chapter of the NAACP, Urban League, Hispanic Center, and a host of others in your area are great sources to connect with. Tapping into college and university fraternities, sororities, and student unions is another way to grow your multiethnicity. Being intentional about increasing your social networks goes a long way in expanding your recruiting pipeline. This is why it's of great importance to get connected to your local community. If you explore this well, you'll find all kinds of new recruiting pipelines to tap into.

One of the organizations we at Lumbermen's have partnered with is the Urban League of West Michigan. Not only have we expanded our recruiting efforts through them, but we've also participated in a couple of events, including mock interviews with youth. This event connected several white people from our organization with black and brown people in the community. This might seem insignificant, but connecting white people with those who are non-white goes a long way toward bridging the gap between racial groups. The closer white people get to where people of color live, work, and play, the more it will help them get comfortable with being around people who are ethnically different from them.

Interviewing

If you want different results, do not do the same things.
—Albert Einstein

I have participated in hundreds of interviews over the years. Most of these were conducted in groups of two or three. I can't tell you how many times I heard someone say, "My gut tells me so-and-so is the best person for the job!" I'm sure his gut has been helpful at times, but when it comes to creating a multiethnic organization, many leaders need to do a gut check.

I remember interviewing an African American female for a customer service job with another white male manager. The candidate had all the qualifications along with strong interpersonal skills. Afterward, the manager said, "She talks kind of loud," and he was hesitant to hire her. I gently suggested it wasn't relevant or a dealbreaker. In the end, we hired her, and she went on to be very successful in multiple positions within the company.

The Gut Check

My point isn't that my colleague had any ill intent. But it certainly was possible that some unconscious idea of his about African Americans informed his knee-jerk reaction to this candidate. Many of us have become successful by "training" our gut to help us make decisions. But we must remember that our "gut" is based on our life experience, including whom we've been exposed to. Your gut may need to learn some new things in order to become more trustworthy on multiethnic hires.

One HR leader told me frankly that the interview process is extremely biased, so we need to examine our processes and eliminate bias where possible. As Jennifer Eberhardt shares in her book *Biased*, "Psychologists today dub [it]... "confirmation bias." People tend to seek out and attend to information that already confirms their beliefs."[32] For instance, hiring decisions are often made based on how much the interviewer resonates with the interviewee. If the candidate shares things in common with the interviewer (where they went to school, the sport they played, the place they grew up, etc.), the interviewer feels more positive toward them. "You play golf? Great!" "You went to the same school my kids attended!" "I know your family. Forest Hills is a great area to live, isn't it?"

Interviews are tricky; in addition to trying to learn relevant information about a candidate, there are a lot of nonverbal and unconscious messages circulating. We're all seeking anything that will guide us toward the right decision. If we're not careful, we perpetuate hiring people just like ourselves. Additionally, we often place too much emphasis on a person's background and experience when the skills needed for most jobs can be trained. Someone might not have the ideal background but have all the characteristics needed to be successful in the job. As the adage goes, "Hire the person, train the skill! If you want a more multiethnic organization, you'll need to be sensitive to how candidates with different ethnic and racial backgrounds are assessed so they're not unwittingly eliminated from the opportunity.

Structured Process Backed by Data

As mentioned earlier, Trinity Health Grand Rapids underwent a major transformation in workplace demographics.[33] How did this happen? They laid the groundwork by enhancing their structured hiring and selection process. What did they enhance? They moved to a data-driven, evidence-based selection process, which was accomplished by adding assessments.

This was a game-changer. The idea was to take the concept of evidence-based medicine and apply it to the hiring process. The CHRO wanted to pursue a process that would greatly minimize bias and stereotypes affecting hiring decisions. So, they embarked on a plan that included measuring both personality and cognitive data. Along with the interview, this information was combined to provide a scoring system that was more of a data-driven approach for selection and hiring. In short, they applied a rating to each assessment and a rating to the structured interview to equitably measure each candidate for job fit. In doing this, they more than doubled their workplace racial diversity over a five-year period.[34]

Here's the thing: They didn't do anything to target more ethnically diverse candidates. All they did was create an evidence-based process that included personality and cognitive data that minimized personal bias. This data was individualized to each candidate and their job fit for the position they were being considered for. As a direct result, they got a more diverse pool of candidates.

Over time, with change management initiatives, the results of using a data-driven approach to selection supported the theory the CHRO had envisioned. Reducing bias and noise in the selection process had a significant impact on who was selected. This became very evident as the candidates being presented were better job fits for what the manager needed in the role.

With any organization, some type of bias impacts the hiring process. Breakthroughs only happen when we're willing to challenge the existing way of doing things. Leaving the process completely to the hiring managers without some sort of structured process and data to drive decisions will likely do little to change your workplace demographics. In many cases, I don't believe managers intentionally leave out minority candidates. However, decisions are often made by the "gut," which is centered on what is familiar to the hiring manager. Maybe the manager will shy away from interviewing candidates with ethnic names, as research has pointed out.[35][36] Maybe a manager will only act on referrals from her sphere of influence. What's clear is that establishing a more structured process that's backed with data goes a long way toward creating a more equitable screening and interview process.

Get More Perspectives

The interview is the number one tool used to determine whether a person is a fit for an open position. Because so much weight is placed on this process, having two or three people interview a candidate is frequently a better practice than interviewing the candidate solo. The perspective another team member has on the candidate provides extra insight a single interviewer might overlook. Having others present during the interview helps neutralize the tendency to hire people just like ourselves. Thoughtfully pairing leaders of color with white leaders can help, too.

Metrics

What gets measured gets done.
—Tom Peters

If we want to improve our organization's performance, we must measure it, and this is equally important when it comes to multiethnic diversity. In order to assess how it's going, we must identify a couple of key metrics. The overarching purpose of these metrics is to track progress over time. Reviewing key metrics periodically helps you assess progress and drive action.

Key metrics to review might include:

1. The number of people of color interviewed for open positions (specifically in the professional ranks). Keep

track of all people interviewed in order to assess this percentage.

2. The number of people of color who make it to the final round of interviews as a percentage of the whole.

3. The number of people of color in your professional ranks. You can certainly tally this number for the rest of your workforce, but the professional role is the one place where racial diversity is often lacking.

4. The number of people of color in leadership.

5. The number of people in your organization (especially leadership) who've participated in racial diversity training (see next chapter).

6. The number of people of color networks the company uses as a channel for recruiting.

You get the point. Regardless of which measures you use, there are simple metrics that can help gauge progress.

Lead vs. Lag

The important thing to note is there are "lead" and "lag" measures, and they both serve a purpose. Lag measures report the results at a given point in time. Annual sales revenue, the temperature in your house, and how much you weigh when stepping on a scale are all examples of a lag metric.

On the other hand, lead measures are predictive and something you can influence. A lead measure for losing ten pounds could be the number of times per week that you exercise. If you consistently exercise five times per week (lead measure), you're likely to move closer to your goal when stepping on the scale (lag measure). The more you pursue a lead measure, the greater chance you have of achieving your goal. This is why identifying and focusing on lead measures is so important. Using our example in the diagram below, your "rock" or lag measure is your weight reduction goal. Your lead measure (lever) for achieving your goal (moving the rock) is exercising five times per week. Another lead measure could be tied to diet. In sum, focusing on lead measures will help you achieve the outcome you desire.

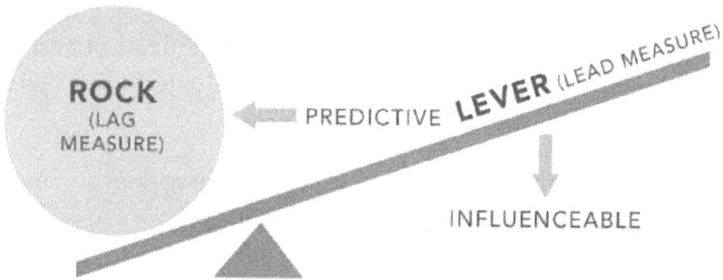

ROCK (LAG MEASURE) ← PREDICTIVE LEVER (LEAD MEASURE) INFLUENCEABLE

(https://strategicdiscipline.positioningsystems.com/blog-0/leading-indicators-influence-and-predict-outcomes)

In an effort to focus on hiring, retention, and workplace demographics, Trinity Health Grand Rapids found it helpful to review one lead and two lag measures monthly. The lead measure was "time to fill" an open position. The more focus they put on this measure, the quicker they were able to increase their percentage of people working in unfilled positions (lag measure). It helped them uncover any barriers that slowed progress toward filling the open spot. The two lag measures tracked were turnover and racial diversity. These two measures may be reporting the news, but they were key indicators that helped them monitor how they were doing in these two important areas. This is why it's important to include both lead and lag measures.

Once, I led the service organization of a manufacturer that sold products through a dealer network. We were trying to figure out a measure that would help improve our dealer's feelings about our service. We decided to have our customer service reps make proactive calls (lead measure) to our dealers as soon as we became aware of problems that impacted our dealers. Making our dealers aware of the problem before it happened immediately improved the perception. Our dealers appreciated the heads-up call as it gave them a few more days to react to the problem.

When we were proactive, our dealers could be proactive and provide better service to their customers. Look to identify a couple of lead measures that will help you become proactive. Tracking at least one or two lead measures will ultimately drive the lag-measure results you're looking for.

Look back at the list of metrics I listed (just after the "Metrics" heading). Can you identify which ones are lead and which ones are lag measures? One lag measure is the number of people of color in the professional ranks of your organization. A lead measure for this is the number of people of color interviewed, along with the number that made it to the final interview round. If the number of people of color interviewed and the number that make it to the final round goes up, the number of people of color hired will likely increase. Targeting lead measures will help you move towards the desired result. So, think through what your lead and lag measures should be, begin tracking, and assess a couple of times a year. Reviewing these metrics semi-annually, at the very least, will help generate healthy dialogue so that action is taken to drive better results.

Don't Let the Metrics Wag the Dog

It's important to remember that metrics are nothing but data points. They serve to facilitate discussion on how the organization is doing in a given area. Eventually, you might find a better metric to focus on. Use the metric review process to not only assess what the metrics are telling you but also if the metrics need to change. Sometimes, we get fixated on attaining a particular number that actually drives the wrong behavior. If the wrong behavior is happening, the tail is wagging the dog, and the metric may need to change.

It's important to understand that the key focal point of what I'm proposing is to bring the best talent to your organization regardless of one's ethnicity or background. This is the end game, so all of these metrics should be supporting this. If you get overly focused on one of these metrics, you can easily drift from what you're trying to accomplish. This is why it's important to periodically assess what the metrics are promoting.

As an example, a manufacturing organization might focus on schedule completion as the main metric to pursue. The problem with being overly focused on this one goal is that quality could be compromised for the sake of completing the schedule. "Don't worry about fixing the minor flaw. Let's just get the product out to meet the schedule!" Do you see how easily you can wander from what you're looking to accomplish? Having a balanced set of metrics that covers a couple of key areas will help you keep the right focus. Remember, numbers are nothing but indicators. They should be interpreted in ways that allow for healthy dialogue that drives the right behavior and positive results.

Retention

We can't stop employees from leaving unless
we have a plan to make them stay!
—Indra Nooyi

It's not going to do you much good to hire ethnically diverse people if they don't find the work environment welcoming. And if you're worried about the costs of becoming multiethnic, just imagine how you're going to feel if you start incurring turnover costs. Leaders of thriving multiethnic teams must be intentional about creating an environment where all ethnicities experience a sense of belonging. Finding ways to create safe spaces for people of color is important.

To start, implement effective training on this subject (see next chapter). If facilitated well, the dialogue throughout the training will help lay the foundation for the culture you're trying to create. Training isn't the end-all, but it's a great starting point in creating an environment that embraces all. In addition, being intentional about having a career development plan for your employees will encourage them to stay. People want to know you're interested in them. The more leaders have conversations with employees about career growth and development, the more engaged they'll be in giving their best. So, keep the focus on developing your employees in order to position them well for organizational opportunities. The more we get to know our diverse employees, the more we'll be rooting for them. Promotional opportunities, just like hiring opportunities, are often built on relationships.

Another way to encourage retention is by having some type of mentor program for racially and ethnically diverse people in your organization. It's important to understand that mentoring doesn't have to be a formal process.

Informally taking time to check in with multiethnic employees goes a long way towards sending the message that "you are welcome here, and we want to see you succeed." Mentors need not be of the same ethnicity (they probably won't be at first). The message and tone are more important; if mentors are sincere in their efforts, employees will feel cared for and supported. Ultimately, leaders must understand that an organization's culture must exhibit a welcoming environment, or you'll quickly lose the very same people you hired.

Lastly, there's one question that could help you understand your culture's treatment of those who are racially diverse. Ask multiethnic and racially diverse people in your organization how comfortable they feel being themselves within the organization. Do they feel a sense of belonging? This will help you uncover how accepting the surrounding culture is and if there's something that needs to change.

Getting Started

1. Assess your attraction, selection, and retention processes. Identify gaps and action to take.

2. Expand your recruiting pipeline to include people of color networks and organizations.

3. Retool your interview and selection process to minimize bias. Train leaders on best practices that level the playing field for all applicants.

4. Identify key metrics that include both lead and lag measures.

5. Take action to develop a more welcoming environment for people coming into the organization—informal or formal mentorships, career development, etc.

CHAPTER FOUR

Employee Engagement

*When people are financially invested, they want a return.
When people are emotionally invested,
they want to contribute.*
—Simon Sinek

Vision + Ownership
Top Leader Buy-in,
Ownership +
Accountability

Process Reset
Revitalized
Attraction,
Selection +
Retention
Processes

Employee
Engagement
Ongoing Training +
Dialogue

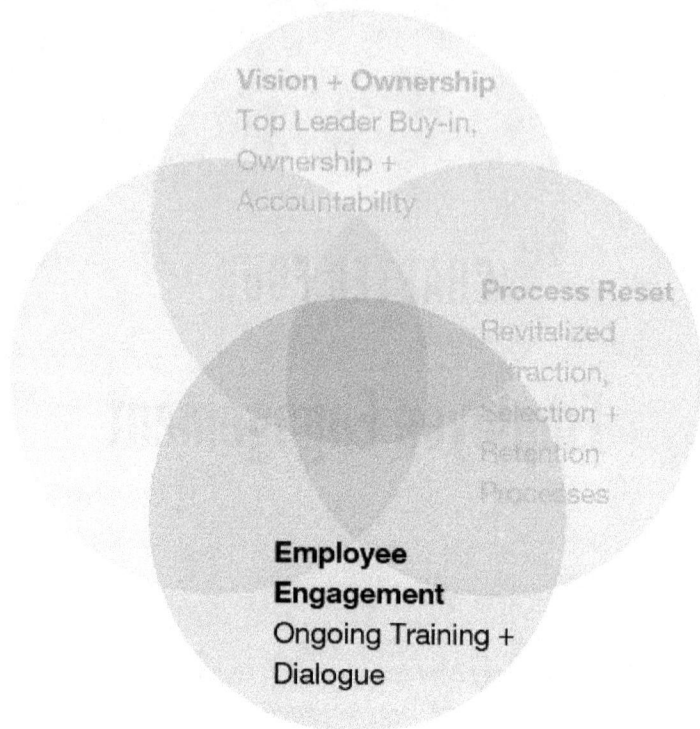

A Different Type of Training

Tell me, and I forget; teach me, and
I may remember; involve me, and I learn.
—Benjamin Franklin

"White people are ignorant! They just don't get it!"
"I can't believe they don't see it!
"This is ridiculous. They need to wake up!"
These are statements I've heard over the years from people of color who are frustrated with the lack of understanding often displayed by whites when it comes to race and racism.

Meanwhile, white people often express frustration about having what they believe is an unnecessary conversation and say things like:

"Why do we have to talk about race issues? Aren't we long past this? Slavery happened many years ago!"

"Everyone has equal opportunity now!"

"This conversation goes nowhere, is fueled by the media, and only gets people upset!"

It's hard to overstate how strongly people feel about this topic. As leaders, we must be careful in how we approach this conversation. Our overarching goal is to create a culture of inclusion that embraces people from different racial and ethnic backgrounds. To accomplish this, training and dialogue must take place in a manner that allows people to honestly reflect on this topic without fear of being labeled, put down, or minimized.

Generally, people want to move forward regarding this topic. But for a lot of people, what that really means is not talking about it. Some want to scrub it from the conversation because they believe it gets us stuck in the past. This is why it's important to clarify that training is not about rehashing the past but learning from it. It's hard to make progress when we don't understand what got us here. And when we paper over what got us here, it can cause people who've experienced racism to dig in further since there's no acknowledgment of the problem. In reality, we get *more stuck* if we're unwilling to look at our history.

This is no different than what occurs between two people in a relationship when there's a severe disagreement. There must be acknowledgment of what happened to pave the way forward. So, the purpose of the training isn't to say we haven't made progress, all white people are racist, and all people of color have been victimized in some way. The purpose is to help people understand what's caused our current reality and recognize that many of our biases have been shaped by our past. And if we don't address this, we will inadvertently hold ourselves back from pursuing a better future that embraces all people.

One important point of clarification: Although we can't ignore the past, we mustn't stay there. If all we do is focus on the past and our problems, we won't make progress. This is why I'm a fan of the concept of appreciative inquiry, where the ultimate focus is not on our problems but on the solutions.[37] It's all about envisioning the way forward and discussing what this looks like. In fact, solution-type questions guided my doctoral research and are the basis for this book. So, we must honestly look at the past to learn from it and then focus our efforts on the way forward.

It's also important to recognize that training on this topic isn't just about critiquing what happened. When this is the tone, many attendees will take a defensive posture, and little, if any, learning will take place. It's not so much criticizing as acknowledging the truth of what transpired and seeking a response that unifies people's understanding of how the past has impacted today.

In any organization, there are two groups of people who need to be trained. Training must begin with the leaders since they will need to model and lead the change. Every leader must fully engage in racial diversity training to ensure what's being promoted is practiced and handled equitably at all levels. Once leadership is trained, the path is cleared to train the rest of the organization.

Training is often viewed as the panacea for anything an organization wants to change, but this is short-sighted. If you're looking to become multiethnic, you must address all four themes treated in this book. Training by itself cannot make the necessary impact. It's a mistake to believe that a one-time discussion will do the trick. For this reason, I use the phrase "ongoing training + dialogue." First and foremost, training on such an important topic *must encourage dialogue.* It must be more than a singular event so people can reflect and digest what's being discussed.

Moreover, it's crucial the facilitator possesses certain skills. Specifically, it's important the facilitator engages those being trained in a healthy conversation. How the training is conducted plays a critical role in creating an environment where people feel comfortable engaging on such a sensitive topic. I think it's also important to clarify at the onset of any training that this is not about the Black Lives Matter (BLM) movement,[38] Critical Race Theory (CRT),[39] or any other ideology being promoted in our society. In fact, this is sometimes why there's such a backlash against current DEI trainings.[40]

When people come to these trainings, they often make assumptions and are concerned why this type of training is taking place. I want to dispel these concerns as quickly as possible. I want them to understand that there's much to learn about this topic without it having anything to do with a political agenda or current movement taking place in our society. For this reason, it's important to help people understand that we're pressing into this topic not because of any movement or ideology but because we believe it will make our organization better. This is simply an opportunity to look at the past and see what we can learn from it. Additionally, it's an opportunity to reflect on our own past and see how we've been affected by it.

Most of us aren't aware of how much our parents have affected our thinking. In talking about the influence our parents have on our racial and ethnic biases, Jennifer Eberhardt comments, "The power of adults to shape that lens is heavily vested in parents. Unsurprisingly, studies confirm that biased parents tend to produce children who are biased as well."[41]

My experience has taught me that the more you engage people in genuine dialogue, the more successful the training will be. The more you ask questions to stimulate honest thought and reflection, the better your chance of moving people toward real change. This is why I use the phrase "a different type of training." The training needs to be geared toward engaging the hearts and minds of the participants being trained. It's not a rote, check-the-box type of training.

As a facilitator, you're looking to stimulate genuine dialogue, transparency, and acknowledgment of the problem. You want people to be comfortable enough in the conversation that they're willing to be misunderstood, and oftentimes, this begins with you. Your willingness to be vulnerable by sharing your own mistakes opens up the conversation for others to contribute and, actually, is a very courageous thing to do. As Brené Brown explains, "Vulnerability is not winning or losing; it's having the courage to show up and be seen when we have no control over the outcome. Vulnerability is not weakness; it's our greatest measure of courage."[42] Being vulnerable often sets the right tone and opens the door for others to engage.

A high-ranking leader at a global company told me that sharing his mistakes allowed other leaders to acknowledge theirs. He went on to say that being honest about his failings was groundbreaking for the organization, as it opened the conversation for genuine dialogue in the leadership ranks. Having leaders share their ignorance and/or mistakes on this topic can be a powerful way to help the rest of the group be honest in their sharing. Encouraging people towards greater self-awareness and being empathetic towards others is what you're aiming for. To do this, you must facilitate in such a way that creates an atmosphere of grace and acceptance.

Grace-Based Training

*Grace is the voice that calls us to change and
then gives us the power to pull it off.*
—Max Lucado

I'll never forget this one anti-racism training. I was excited to be part of the group and looked forward to the training, but then the facilitator showed a video. On the one hand, I personally found the video compelling and emotionally provocative. On the other hand, I recognized that much of it was designed to trigger feelings of shame in white participants. After watching the video, people reacted in a variety of ways. Some got angry; others shed tears. But what became clear was that *the majority of white people simply withdrew from the conversation.*

This is why I'm not a fan of what I call "shame-based" trainings. In fact, there's some evidence to suggest that this type of approach has the opposite effect.[43] The intent is to shock people into facing the reality of the problem—to wake people up from their ignorance. I'm not against people feeling uncomfortable when they face their biased assumptions; I care too much about seriously moving this conversation forward to say people shouldn't ever feel bad. In fact, feeling a bit disturbed may be the very thing that brings about a new perspective.

I also acknowledge that many white people shy away from this conversation because it forces them to deal with the ugliness of racism when they prefer to ignore it. It makes them feel uncomfortable largely because they've never had to engage in or think about this topic and partly because they don't want to believe it's true. Their lived experience may be very different, so how could these incidents really happen? When confronted with the topic, the tendency for many whites is to dismiss it. Although the phrase is often mis-applied, "white fragility" is a real thing. Let's be honest; all people are fragile when confronted with truths they'd rather not discuss. However, *people will never move from discomfort to personal change if they feel under attack.*

"I was nervous about this training."

"I was afraid I was going to get beat up again."

"I've attended trainings where it's a white beat-up session."

These are real comments from people after I conducted a racial diversity training. Just the sound of "diversity train-ing" strikes fear in many white people because they've felt ambushed in past trainings. I can't emphasize this point enough. Creating an environment that allows people to express real feelings without fear of being emotionally battered pro-vides the best environment for transformational change.

"It's all sensationalized and politicized."

"The media only makes it worse."

"It's nothing but people talking past each other with no real solution."

These statements reflect the frustration many feel about the topic. Since what's largely demonstrated from media sources leads to more heat than light, many are turned off. They view it as a no-win conversation that only leads to angry feelings and emotional exhaustion. Who wants to enter into a conversation like this?

Let's be honest and acknowledge that conscious racial prejudice has fallen since the 1960s. This is the point many white people make when feeling there's no need for training. However, this doesn't mean that prejudice is no longer an issue and doesn't play itself out in the workplace. In reality, there's a more subtle type of prejudice that's unconscious and influences on-the-job behaviors and decisions. Research indicates that this unconscious type of racial prejudice hasn't declined nearly as much as the conscious type. In practice, it does affect our hiring and promotion decisions. The truth is that implicit bias resides in all people as well as in organizational systems, so having a plan to address both is critical.[44]

My research suggests that training needs to be "grace-based." The phrase used by one high-level leader I interviewed who completed his own doctoral dissertation on this topic was "grace and repair." This leader went on to explain that the climate you want to strive for in your training is one that allows people to express themselves fully without being condemned. If a white person makes an ignorant statement, the response shouldn't be to stigmatize the person. Instead, it should be sensitively addressed in a manner that encourages greater self-awareness around the topic. Instead of wagging a finger, the response should be one that leads people to deeper reflection. At the same time, you sensitively address ignorance by helping them see the other side. This is "grace and repair."

"This topic is a waste of time!" says a participant. "We're long past any real race issue, and if people want to get ahead, all they have to do is apply themselves."

"Well," the facilitator says, "that's interesting. I respect your opinion and acknowledge that all of us play a major role in how our lives turn out. But is it possible that the hiring process may unknowingly encourage more white candidates to join the organization than people of color? Is it possible that if an organization is largely white when it comes to the interview process, it might not cast its recruiting net wide enough to attract people of color? Is it possible that our networks only encompass people who are largely white and missing out on some great candidates? And is it possible that some white people have a bias that affects who they might hire?"

This is an example of a conversation I've had with people who don't believe that race plays a role today. You can take this conversation in a lot of directions, but what's important is to acknowledge where the person is coming from and ask questions to get them to think deeper. I could've chosen to rebuke the person for their ignorance, but this ultimately works against what you're trying to accomplish. You can't force people to believe something. You can't guilt people into believing what you want them to believe. But you can get them to reflect deeper on the topic in order to help them perceive that there may be merit to your perspective. This is grace and repair in action.

On a further note, it might be best to have a one-to-one follow-up session with the individual. In doing this, you turn the public spotlight off, which allows them to be more open and transparent. At the end of the day, you're not looking for outward compulsion but inner conviction.

If the conversation gets a little heated or you sense people are having a hard time with the topic, it's likely best to encourage them to reflect on it without feeling the need to comment. What you're trying to encourage is greater self-awareness around biases related to race and ethnicity, and this will only happen if people take time to self-reflect. As Jennifer Eberhardt comments in *Biased*, "I also recognized that the capacity for growth comes from our willingness to reflect, to probe in search of some actionable truth."[45]

As shown, grace and repair doesn't leave ignorant or offensive comments unchallenged. Instead, the facilitator actively cultivates an environment that allows people to express their thoughts freely while addressing the sensitive issue. This is a challenging task for the facilitator, as some people refuse to understand the other side. However, if handled well, the conversation may be the very thing that unlocks unconscious bias for many participants.

A white woman approached me in private after a training. She said that she appreciated the training and wanted to let me know that, occasionally, she has bad thoughts about black people. The training brought these feelings to the surface, and she recognized her need to deal with these thoughts. This may seem like a small breakthrough, but if you think about it, it is quite profound, given the 90-minute training.

People have all kinds of wrong-headed thoughts about race. And here in the workplace, this lady's insight came to life. I'm not so naïve to think that this woman has overcome her racial biases. But becoming more self-aware is a great place to start. Think about it. Her unconscious bias was exposed as she came to the realization that even she had these thoughts. This woman is likely to treat people of color differently in the workplace and her community. A small but significant change.

It's also important to create an environment of acceptance for people of color. It's not uncommon for a black or brown person to share stories of racism and get angry over the past. It's critical that the facilitator acknowledges their experience and makes it safe for them to share their story. Acknowledging the felt pain is crucial to creating a safe environment for heartfelt sharing.

White people often dismiss what's said when they don't feel it's truly race-related. In some cases, they might be right. But in other cases, race has truly been at play so it's important to encourage people to fully comprehend the other side. If nothing else, it can be helpful to point out that oftentimes, a black person has to live with the constant question of whether they are being treated differently because of their race in a way that their white peers do not.

Two years ago in the city where I reside, a black Congolese young adult was shot and killed by a white police officer during a scuffle.[46] Many in the black community were instantly aware of what happened and were highly upset. On the flip side, many in the white community initially knew very little about the incident and, when the video was released, quickly ran to the defense of the policeman. The different reactions to this tragedy highlight the deep chasm in viewpoints that is only bridged by engaging each other in honest dialogue.

Years ago, I met weekly with teenage urban youth as part of a church outreach program. Over fifteen years, I drove through the heart of urban neighborhoods and never once was pulled over by the police. I had a friend who also did this work who was a person of color. I couldn't begin to tell you how many times he was pulled over in the years we worked together—one time when we were talking on the phone! He acknowledged that sometimes there was a good reason for this, but most of the time, the reason given was nothing more than "You're a suspicious-looking character."

Listening to a person's painful story may be the very thing that opens our eyes to the reality of what is experienced. The more that people listen, acknowledge, and engage in these conversations, the more their understanding will grow. Over time, it becomes less "my opinion versus your opinion" and more "we understand each other, we can learn from each other, and we are in this together."

When it comes to these discussions, it's important to avoid stereotyping. This may seem obvious, but we often make assumptions that all white or black people feel a certain way when they don't. White people oftentimes think that if a black person makes a comment about an issue, they're speaking for all black people. Although there might be experiences common to a particular race or ethnicity, not everyone feels the same.

During one training I conducted, an African American man expressed his opinion that today's diversity trainings are causing young people of color to presume racism is rampant and hindering their ability to get ahead. He was very much against the anti-racism type trainings that are happening in many educational institutions. He believes they encourage a victim mindset, which can lead people to feel powerless, hamper self-motivation, and do more harm than good. The reality is that there are other African Americans who would disagree with him and believe that training is necessary to help people understand real issues surrounding the historical reality of racism in our country.

Here's the other challenge: If people of color express concern that these trainings promote victimhood, white people often feel justified in dismissing the conversation entirely. All of these nuances are valid matters that we must be sensitive to. It also reinforces what the purpose of this conversation needs to be about—to help all of us uncover biases that might be getting in the way of how we think about and treat people who are ethnically and racially different.

When training, it's important that the group size is not too large. Once you get over 10–12 people, you're running the risk of losing engagement from some who will sit on the sidelines. There are ways to facilitate larger group trainings, but you must be thoughtful in how you do this and look for ways to cultivate smaller conversations within the larger group (break into pairs, etc.).

When I facilitate a training, I'm looking to help people be as real with themselves as possible. It's not easy, but it's what's needed to get beyond the surface. Most people already have their guard up in an ordinary group setting, much less a group that's discussing a difficult topic. Most people don't want to look bad in front of others and easily get caught up in trying to say the right thing. For this reason, I attempt to promote an environment that encourages people to think deeply about this topic and identify their real thoughts. No one is forced to share the uncomfortable thoughts they may find in themselves. But when people open up, I attempt to model how to affirm their courage and vulnerability, acknowledge their experience with grace, and, if necessary, reframe and repair.

If you actively cultivate a welcoming environment where people feel comfortable sharing what's in their hearts without fear of being shamed or harshly criticized, you've created the best environment for change. This is why I state in my training, "This is a safe place to share. You won't be condemned for saying the wrong thing." It's in a climate of openness and acceptance that people will most likely share their true feelings. And when they share their true feelings, the door is now open for real change.

History

History, despite its wrenching pain, cannot be unlived,
but if faced with courage, need not be lived again.
—Maya Angelou

"I was never taught that. I'm shocked this happened so recently!" I can't tell you how many times I've heard this during a training. One of the greatest barriers to the race conversation is not knowing history. People need to understand that our present-day racial disparities didn't happen by chance. Without understanding our history, we're left with incomplete stories, hearsay from friends and media, and personal assumptions we've made. We tell ourselves stories that are ill-informed, which makes it very difficult to move forward. Working with bad information won't inspire change. But filling in the historical gaps often evokes people's internal sense of justice and morality.

It's very important to include a section on the history of race in America when doing the training. If a person believes our history has been largely fair to all people and our faults have been relatively minor and over and done with, there will be little understanding and engagement on this topic. Again, the purpose of this is not to shame or dredge up past negativity about anyone's race. And it's not to condemn our country as if we're the only one to have done something terribly wrong. But many of us grow up with a sugar-coated version of our national history.

There's an ugliness to our record that must be shared. The purpose of doing so is to help people understand how we arrived at where we are today. You could go in a lot of directions when discussing history, but I've found it best to keep the focus on several little-known facts about the last century. Let me explain why.

Everyone knows that slavery took place in this country many years ago, but they tend to believe it's no longer relevant to the present. So, I focus on a few obscure details that help reframe that understanding.

Although some form of slavery has existed since the beginning of time, most don't realize there are differences in slave models. Many who became enslaved in other societies were considered indentured servants. This model sometimes involved the element of choice, and, most importantly, the servant was set free after a set number of years. Although there were some indentured servants in America, by and large, American slavery took on a different form, which is referred to as *chattel slavery*. Under this definition, one person has total ownership of another, and in America, it was for their entire life.

Christopher Columbus laid the groundwork for slavery during his first voyage in 1492. When he found how "docile" the native inhabitants were in the West Indies, the explorer began to see them as potential servants. He wrote in his log, "They ought to be good servants of good intelligence."[47] But instead of hiring them, Columbus enslaved a number of the people from the islands he visited. Fast forward to late August 1619, when we have the first recorded instance of the trade of African people in what would become the United States. It eventually took the ratification of the 13th Amendment to officially end the institution of chattel slavery in the United States in December of 1865.

Another piece of information worth sharing is that the word *race* is a social construct.[48] It's a human-invented classification system. Race is not biological. There is no gene or cluster of genes common to all black or white people. The term *race*, used infrequently before the 1500s, was used to identify groups of people with a kinship or group connection. The modern-day use of the term *race*, identifying groups of people by physical traits, appearance, or characteristics, has been used to justify inequality.

Racial classification in the United States started in the 1700s with three ethnically distinct groups: White Europeans, Native Americans, and Africans.[49] The categorization was often used to assure whites they were superior to the people they were mistreating. Without going into any greater detail, sharing this history helps people understand how racism developed throughout our country.

After sharing these facts, I spend the bulk of the time helping people understand what happened after 1865. I begin with the period of Reconstruction and then go into a conversation about the period of white backlash referred to as Redemption (beginning in 1877), which laid the groundwork for Jim Crow.[50] There's little understanding of the systemic racism that was rampant in the 1900s. For this reason, I find it highly beneficial to provide a historical overview of what happened in the 20th century. In particular, I draw attention to the post-World War II period.

In the aftermath of W.W. II, a housing boom occurred that was stimulated by the G.I. Bill. Passed by Congress in 1944, the G.I. Bill was designed to assist returning W.W. II veterans. Benefits included low-cost mortgages, low-interest loans to start a business or farm, one year of unemployment compensation, and dedicated payments of tuition and living expenses to attend high school, college, or vocational school. These benefits were available to all veterans who had been on active duty during the war years for at least 90 days and had not been dishonorably discharged.

Unfortunately, many people of color were left out. In the New York and northern New Jersey suburbs, 67,000 mortgages were insured by the G.I. Bill, but fewer than 100 were taken out by non-whites.[51] Banks and mortgage agencies often refused loans to black people, making the G.I. Bill even less effective for African Americans. Redlining was also rampant at this time, where a loan or insurance was refused to people who lived in certain areas deemed to be a poor financial risk. Unfortunately, the areas redlined were exactly where the highest percentage of people of color lived.

The bottom line is there were a slew of discriminatory practices instituted by local, state, and federal agencies that many people today are unaware of. Ask people to consider how important education and home ownership have been to their family in the last 100 years, and they will begin to see how this is relevant to the conversation.

Another reality that many people have either forgotten or never understood is that when the Civil Rights legislation of the 1960s took place, there was more white backlash. Similar to "redemption" after slavery, there were a number of white Americans, particularly in the South, who became recalcitrant. They strongly opposed desegregation and made it difficult for progress to occur.[52]

If possible, it's best to tie this history directly to the city your organization resides in. In most cities, there's enough historical data (books, articles, etc.) that will help paint a clear picture of the patterns that developed because of these practices.[53] Sharing this level of detail brings the point home even more. In my case, I've been able to help people understand why, even today, over 50% of African Americans live in a particular square block in our city.

As I unpack the effects of all the discriminatory practices that severely limited African American's ability to purchase homes in the suburbs, people often have a "lightbulb" moment. They begin to see how these practices set in motion policy and wrongheaded ideas that directly tie to the racial discord we still have today. In essence, the systems that were created to keep racial minorities down have an after-effect that we're still recovering from.

We need to recognize that there are problems and tensions in our society today that are a hangover from years of racist policy and practice. This in no way denies the great progress made over the years, but we must recognize the fallout from past unjust practices.

One of my sons mentioned to me that every time race was brought up in school, it highlighted the negative. It made him uncomfortable as many in a mostly white school turned their eyes toward him. He made it very clear to me how important it is to share the positive contributions of people of color throughout the years. Everyone needs to understand that despite what happened, many were able to excel and make significant contributions to our society. This accomplishes two things.

For one, it reminds people of the profound impact made by those who were discriminated against. Secondly, despite the horrific racism and poor treatment, it's inspiring to realize that people of color were able to rise above the challenges of their day. Only a strong people can organize, play a key role in shaping our society, and victoriously advance despite extreme oppression. In essence, it's a story about the two sides of humanity. On the one hand, it demonstrates how cruel people can be in striving to maintain an advantage over another. On the other hand, it demonstrates how a united people can overcome any odds, no matter how bad the situation.

To further clarify, there are two stories to tell when it comes to the history of race in America, and one is actually positive. There are many examples of people who overcame racial injustice that should inspire all of us. This isn't to lessen the blow of the devastating effects of racism but to remind us that there are many lessons to be learned from this struggle for equality. For one, the racism experienced in our country has lasting consequences that are being felt even today. Another lesson is that all of us can be proud of those who persevered and triumphed despite the odds being stacked against them. If anything, this should motivate us to continue our efforts to create an environment that is fair and equitable for all people.

Unconscious Bias

*To know the true reality of yourself, you must be aware not
only of your conscious thoughts but also of your
unconscious prejudices, bias, and habits.*
—Unknown

I was twenty-four years old, hoping to make a little extra
money by delivering packages for UPS during the Christmas
season. I was the "runner"—the person who teamed with a
driver to deliver the package. It was my job to bring the packages up to the front door, ring the doorbell, and head back
to the brown delivery truck. Being competitive, I decided
to literally run to and from each drop-off to see how many
packages we could deliver in a day. To our satisfaction, we
actually broke the record for the most packages delivered in
one day.

My driver was a white woman of around thirty. During
the course of one conversation, she confided to me, "I hate
black people." Surprised by her out-of-the-blue hostility, I
asked, "Why?" She proceeded to tell me that she hated black
people because her sister was raped by a black man. "So," I
asked, "If a white guy raped your sister, would you hate all
white people?" She didn't say much after this, but about a
week later, she said to me, "You know… you got me thinking. I guess it's wrong to hate all black people because of the
actions of one black man."

Many people don't realize the hidden reasons behind
their feelings. Many are unconscious as to what's triggering
certain thoughts when they see a person of another ethnicity. I like the term *unconscious bias* (also called implicit
bias) because everyone can relate to it. It's a term that puts
all of us on a level playing field. Unconscious biases are

learned stereotypes that are automatic, unintentional, deeply ingrained, universal, and able to influence behavior.

We all have them, which is why we need training to help us understand our biases and the impact they have. Done well, such training will tease out some of the unconscious biases that we each possess and can cause us to rule out or overlook great candidates for positions and promotions. It will help us understand any fear, ignorance, misperception, or prejudice we might have and promote greater understanding and togetherness for everyone in our organization. Helping people understand their biases creates greater self-awareness, which increases the odds of transformational growth.

Empathy...Going Deeper

You can only understand people if you feel them in yourself.
—John Steinbeck

When you show deep empathy toward others, their defensive energy goes down, and positive energy replaces it. That's when you can get more creative in solving problems.
—Stephen Covey

Sympathy is when you feel bad or sorry for another person. Empathy is when you imagine yourself in another's shoes enough to feel *with* them, even if you've never shared the same experience. In multiethnic training, you're trying to stimulate a greater appreciation of different perspectives. While we can never understand precisely what another goes through, in our humanness, we can still perceive the experiences others have. We can't change people's deep-down feelings with a one-time training or conversation, but we can help people reach a place where they empathize in ways they didn't before. This is how the process of change begins at the human level.

Again, it's "ongoing training + dialogue." It must be *ongoing* in the sense that it's intentionally discussed more than once, especially within the leadership ranks. Transformation happens over a period of time, so we must keep the conversation going in healthy ways for the organization to gain real traction. One way to do this is to break up the training into a couple of segments over a year or two. It also could be done by calling people together to discuss recent events where race problems have been exposed. Maybe it's an agenda item for your staff meeting. Regardless of what you do, it's important to remember that you can't move through this quickly. It's a dialogue and process you commit to for the long haul.

Real change only happens if there's genuine dialogue. One-sided discussions only take you so far. Ensuring there's real dialogue means that both sides are engaging in the discussion in an open manner, which creates the best climate for change. It's in the dialogue—not a monologue—that seeds of transformation are planted. It's in the dialogue—not a presentation—where real opportunities exist to plumb the depths of thought so that real change begins.

One important point: Generally, people can only take so much of a conversation that evokes strong feelings. Some people like to engage in going deeper, while others do not. For this reason, it might be best to avoid going deep when you sense the environment is not ready for it. In fact, it's likely best to walk through the facts and channel the conversation around the broader topic of bias since this is something everyone can relate to.

In summary, the critical pieces to creating employee engagement are having an effective facilitator and then investing the time for ongoing training + dialogue. The more you can help people be honest with their thoughts and feelings while creating an environment of grace and forgiveness, the better the climate will be for transformational change.

Getting Started

1. Ensure you have a good facilitator who seeks to create a safe space for training participants.

2. Work towards honest, healthy dialogue in an environment of grace.

3. Ensure a high-level history is shared, highlighting the systemic injustices of the past century. Remember: the purpose of this step is not to critique but to acknowledge what's transpired.

4. Tied to the above, share local history to help people clearly see the impact on the local community.

5. Encourage people to explore their unconscious biases regarding race and ethnicity.

6. Encourage participants to grow in their empathy towards each other.

CHAPTER FIVE

Inspiration + Guidance

*You just have to have the guidance to lead you in the
direction until you can do it yourself.*
—Tina Yothers

Vision + Ownership
Top Leader Buy-In,
Ownership +
Accountability

Inspiration + Guidance
Use of Coach,
Guiding Team +
Debriefing

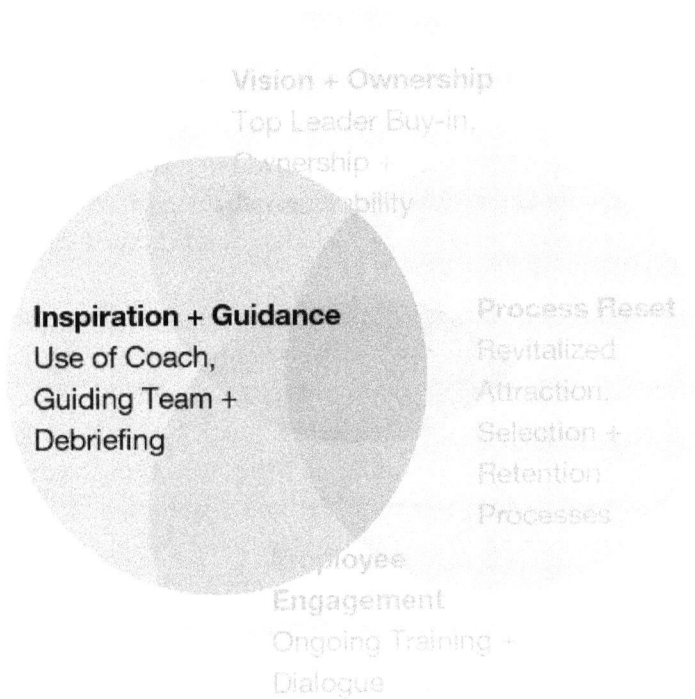

Process Reset
Revitalized
Attraction,
Selection +
Retention
Processes

Employee
Engagement
Ongoing Training +
Dialogue

Coaches

Thank you for pointing me in the right direction.
—Thank you note to a coach

The leader of a global organization told me about the great racial and ethnic progress made in his organization over the last 10 years. He said they couldn't have accomplished this without the help of a guy who served as his coach. This coach helped him navigate the challenges and encouraged him along the way.

The last sphere in this model is entitled "inspiration + guidance." This chapter will be much shorter than the others but will highlight a couple of key points. For organizations to maintain momentum after starting down the path of multiethnicity, there must be something that drives the plan forward. Normal day-to-day business challenges keep organizations focused on what they need to do to succeed in their area of expertise.

In striving to achieve a multiethnic organization, there aren't the normal prompts to keep momentum going. In fact, the regular daily challenges do nothing but pull the leader's attention away from the multiethnic goal. For this reason, it's of extreme importance to enlist the use of an inside or outside coach to ensure the multiethnic plan moves forward. As one leader said to me, "You have to find someone to come alongside you to do this well." So, it's critical to your success to have someone guide you through the process. Without the proper guidance, you won't make the progress you desire.

Identifying a coach can be accomplished in a couple of ways. It's ideal if you have someone on the executive leadership team who has a passion for this topic. This person, if not the CEO or president, can work closely with top leaders to ensure the plan is pursued and stays at the forefront of organizational conversations. Having the coach as a member of the executive team is optimal as it ensures the conversation continues despite daily organizational challenges.

Another way to go about this is to identify someone in your organization who acts as the "champion" of this initiative. If no one in the executive ranks possesses a passion for ethnic diversity, you could look for someone in your organization who does. My only caution is that if this person isn't in top leadership, their influence might not be great enough to keep it at the forefront of executive conversations. In this case, it would be up to the executive team to ensure this person gets the support and attention needed to drive the initiative forward. Remember, if it's not owned at the top, it won't go anywhere.

I worked for an organization where a high-level leader fully bought into an important operations initiative. He and his team were all in. To implement the idea, he selected a non-leader in the organization he deemed the "champion" of what we were trying to accomplish. The executive and his team gave the champion their full support. This led to the initiative gaining traction and ultimately succeeding. So, it can be done, but it needs strong backing from top leadership to be successful.

The positive of having an inside coach is that they understand the culture and have the know-how to navigate the organizational nuances. However, if there isn't someone who fits this role, it would be wise to enlist the help of an outside coach. An outside coach not only helps keep you on track but will oftentimes bring a wealth of ideas. They often bring a fresh and unique perspective - reinforcing the goal of this process within the process itself. Many of these coaches have worked with other organizations. These learnings can point you in the right direction. Regardless of how it works best for you, the use of an internal or external coach will ensure the organization is guided toward the desired results.

One important point to consider. Please take time to reflect on what I'm about to say over the next couple of paragraphs before reacting to the point being made. Many white leaders look to have a person of color champion the idea from the inside or be the coach from the outside. This is great if you find the right person. White leaders need to learn and gather insight from those who are close to the issue. Getting input through a survey to people of color in your organization or conducting focus groups can help. Listen well, be willing to get uncomfortable, seek to understand the issues, and be accountable for taking action. In essence, it's all about leveraging the data and fixing the systems—understanding the issues and addressing the cause.

As white leaders engage people of color in this work, they will begin to appreciate the challenges DEI practitioners face. There will be a greater desire to focus resources and provide accountability that strengthens the overall culture of the organization. However, the tendency for many white leaders is to hastily bring in a person of color (to speak, consult, lead the charge, etc.), assuming they're the ones who need to lead this conversation. If you're not careful, you unknowingly undercut what's critical to the success of your efforts. Why do I say this? Simply because there's a very important nuance to consider.

For any multiethnic journey to succeed, it must be owned by the top leader(s) of the organization. If we're quick to designate the topic to someone simply because they're a person of color, we could abdicate our role of ownership. In reality, we might perpetuate what we're trying to change. We put it on the person of color to orchestrate rather than own and figure out what needs to be done as a white leader to move forward. We sit on the sidelines, feeling we don't have a seat at the table when we have an important contribution to make. This is very subtle, but it's the difference between leading the charge yourself on a critical business initiative to ensure it takes root or turning it over to someone else.

If you lead the charge, there's no question about its importance. If it's important enough, you need to own it. Again, white leaders need to get input from people of color to understand the issues, but they should never abdicate their role of owning and leading the charge.

Let me tease this out a little more. If the best person to act as a coach or champion for multiethnic diversity is a person of color, you—as a white leader—need to make sure you're partnering with this person. Work closely with them to understand the issues and provide the support needed. At the same time, you must fully own the initiative and outcome yourself.

On the other hand, if you don't have a person of color acting as your coach, this can be equally good if this person has a good grasp of the issues. In one sense, this demonstrates what you're looking to accomplish. You're demonstrating to the organization that this issue matters regardless of one's race or ethnicity. In reality, you're setting a great example by proving that a white leader can own and speak to this issue. By leading the charge as a white person, you're pressing into where we want to go—a place where all people lean into bridging our racial and ethnic gap. This sends a powerful message to the entire organization.

Here's my point. If the white leader doesn't fully own the initiative, it will not have staying power. As soon as the organization experiences trouble (loss of market share, major operational challenges...), the multiethnic program becomes an easy target to cut. Ultimately, whether you have a person of color providing guidance or not, white leaders need to fully own the plan. When white leaders take the reins, it's no longer a topic relegated to the sidelines. It's no longer the optional appetizer and becomes the main course. Most indispensably, you become effective in knowing what to do because you learn from owning and engaging on this topic. At the end of the day, it sends a strong message to everyone in the organization that this isn't a black or people of color thing; it's a human thing. This is how it works its way into the DNA of your organization.

Guiding Team + Debriefing

Never doubt that a small group of thoughtful,
committed citizens can change the world;
indeed, it's the only thing that ever has.
—Margaret Mead

One of the things you'll want to do early on in your multi-ethnic journey is form a guiding team. This cohort should be comprised of people who are part of the executive team and others at various levels within the organization. The main purpose of this team is to make sure your efforts gain traction.

Peter Thiel (entrepreneur billionaire who cofounded PayPal) says that an ideal board size for an organization is three.[54] This may sound inadequate, but I wholeheartedly concur with the thought behind what he's saying. The best teams are of a smaller size, although admittedly, three might be too small. I have no formula for what the exact number should be. However, when you form a team focused on this topic, keep it to a size that allows you to discuss the issues, understand the impact on the organization, and take action. Nothing is more frustrating than having a team meeting that lacks focus and doesn't drive action. If you want to set yourself up for success, keep the size small and ensure a meeting facilitator executes a good agenda that drives results.

Once the team has been formed, it's important that members meet regularly enough to keep the momentum going. The team doesn't need to meet weekly and may not even need to meet monthly, but make certain you're meeting frequently enough to keep things moving. If it's infrequent, momentum will die as people's mindshare gets consumed by other work-related items. Meeting every other month is likely a good rhythm to gain real traction and keep positive energy flowing.

It's also important that this team debriefs periodically. Debriefing is crucial for navigating this challenging journey. There will be strong feelings on all sides surrounding this topic, so it's important to dig into what you're hearing and feeling. Debrief how the training is going. Debrief if progress is being made. And, crucially, debrief anything that's not going well.

Any key initiative is going to have its challenges and setbacks. Make time to have candid conversations with each other. Sometimes, there are adjustments to make, and other times, it's just a matter of airing out feelings with no need for action. In doing this, the direction to take and adjustments that need to be made will become clearer. Additionally, celebrate progress. If there's one thing I hear from leaders frequently, it's that we don't do a good job of celebrating small wins, so keep the positive developments in front of people. One important note: Don't let someone's strong opinion derail progress. Accept the fact that feelings run the gamut on this topic. Hear them out and discern what to learn, but don't let them stop you from moving forward.

Associations & Networks

If you want to go somewhere, it is best to find
someone who has already been there.
—Robert Kiyosaki

Seek out associations and networks that share your multiethnic values. There are all kinds of ideas you can learn about by being connected to these networks. When you go down the multiethnicity path, you will run into many obstacles. Your vision will help you persevere, and the buy-in at all levels will give you resilience, but often, your network will have the experience and perspective that can help you make the necessary adjustments. There's much we can learn from others that will help us avoid making common mistakes. Not only can the shared content be rich, but conversations with people who are part of these networks might provide great insight as you journey toward a multiethnic organization.

Getting Started

1. Identify your key inside or outside coach, if not you.

2. Create a guiding team to ensure follow-through of the plan.

3. Ensure a good meeting agenda and establish the frequency of meetings.

4. Ensure regular debriefing takes place so that key learnings are baked into future plans.

5. Identify associations or networks that will help inspire and guide you towards your vision.

CHAPTER SIX

Applying the Best Practices: A Case Study

People say there are two kinds of learning: experience, which is gained from your own mistakes, and wisdom, which is learned from the mistakes of others.
—John Maxwell

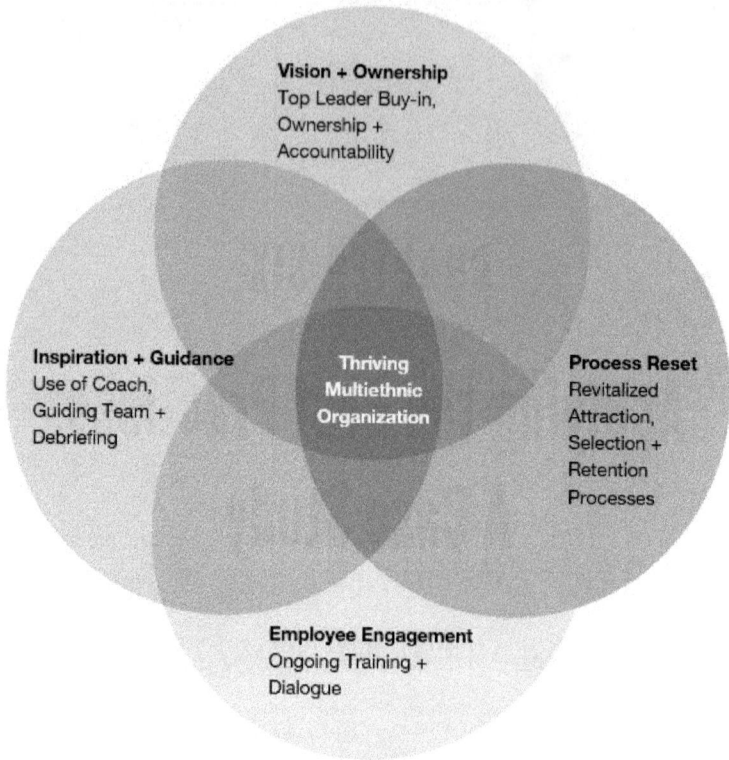

Vision + Ownership
Top Leader Buy-in,
Ownership +
Accountability

Inspiration + Guidance
Use of Coach,
Guiding Team +
Debriefing

**Thriving
Multiethnic
Organization**

Process Reset
Revitalized
Attraction,
Selection +
Retention
Processes

Employee Engagement
Ongoing Training +
Dialogue

L umbermen's, Inc. is a Midwest distributor of building materials and manufacturer/fabricator of entry doors, laid-up panels, and stone and solid surface products. It is 100% employee-owned (ESOP), with sales over $400 million and approximately 650 employee-owners. The following case study will help you understand how we got started, where we are today, and how you can navigate your multiethnic journey.

Top-Level Buy-in

I joined Lumbermen's, Inc. in July of 2019 as a vice president and member of the executive team. I was fortunate that the president of the company took an interest in my doctoral research and gave his full support to implement many of my ideas. After gaining alignment with our president, I was given the opportunity to share these ideas with the executive leadership team, who fully supported the concept. After gaining executive support, I met with our HR leader to get her thoughts and buy-in. Again, there was complete support in helping our organization become more multiethnic and racially diverse.

Sounds easy, right? It's true it won't be as easy as this for everyone. You can't control whether or not people will buy in, but you can control how you ask for their buy-in. When you approach the issue assuming everyone wants to do the right thing rather than criticizing what they've already done, people are more likely to respond well. It doesn't have to be a battle.

Initially, I set up two focus groups: one with people of color and the other with white people. The purpose of this was to gain insight into how these two groups felt about intentionally moving towards greater multiethnic diversity. I conducted these focus groups as part of my doctoral research and received welcoming feedback from both groups.

Process Reset

With the focus group data in mind, we drafted a rough plan of action that was approved by all members of the executive team. We took two immediate actions. First, we committed to intentionally expanding our recruiting pipelines to include more candidates of color without compromising our hiring standards. I mention not "compromising our standards" because this is what many people are concerned about when moving in this direction. We were very clear from the outset that there wouldn't be any type of quota system when it came to hiring. We knew any hint of this would create morale issues surrounding our initiative. Frankly, regardless of one's ethnicity, very few people are interested in quotas, and no one wants to be considered a "diversity hire." What is desired is equal opportunity to compete for a job, and that's what becoming more multiethnic is all about.

Employee Engagement

The second action we pursued was racial diversity training geared towards high-level leaders within the organization. At the time, we had 30+ people who fit the bill. I facilitated a two-hour training that covered many of the principles I've shared in this book. The training kicked off with an introduction from the president, who gave his full support for what we were doing.

I structured the training by first facilitating a discussion around our company's mission, vision, and promise (MVP) statements. We had a great initial discussion as we unpacked what these statements were all about. Starting off with your mission, vision, and values statements is a great way to introduce the topic of racial diversity.

In Lumbermen's case, we ended up changing our mission statement to the following: "We exist to enrich the lives of people by intentionally caring for all who experience us." This made for an easy tie into why we were promoting this topic, as it helped employees see how it fit within the organization's values. Early in the training, I asked our leaders to gather in groups of two to three and discuss their initial reaction to this subject. I wanted to flush out any feelings on the topic early in the conversation. I then walked through a historical piece on race in America that emphasized what happened in the last century.

After sharing this historical lens, I walked through a brief history of our company. Lumbermen's began in 1955. It was birthed as a business that benefited from the post-World War II housing boom. Lumbermen's got its start partly due to programs in place that encouraged home ownership. However, the facts clearly show that while whites dramatically benefited from these programs (G.I. Bill, etc.), the black community was severely restricted in accessing these benefits. Access to loans and capital, access to popular suburban neighborhoods, and access to quality education were limited largely to the white population. Essentially, our company got a great kick-start due to programs and policies that largely benefited those who were white.

At this point in the training, I shared history related to our city—the good and the bad. While the city of Grand Rapids and the surrounding West Michigan area has much to boast about (great place to raise a family, lots of philanthropy, high median income level...), it hasn't benefited everyone the same. When you look at our city's historical impact on African Americans, you get a completely different picture. On the one hand, it's been touted as a great place to raise a family. On the other, it's been dubbed the second worst city in America for African Americans economically.[55] So, we spent time in the training exploring this dichotomy.

As I unpacked local and company history, there were lots of great conversations that took place. Most importantly, many people commented that they didn't realize much of what happened last century. It's very important that the facilitator of these conversations encourages dialogue while allowing time for personal reflection. If facilitated well, people identify important insights that help move an organization forward. Consequently, everyone was forming a new appreciation and perspective on the topic of racial diversity.

At our next executive team meeting, we discussed the action steps that were necessary to keep the momentum going. We decided it was important to conduct training for next-level leaders so that every leader in the company was educated on this topic. After all of our leaders were trained, we started the process of training for every employee in the company.

Inspiration + Guidance

After conducting the leader training, we formed a team that would help keep the fire alive and guide the future direction of this initiative. The group was comprised of the president, our HR leader, a former executive who has strong ties to the urban community, two African American leaders, and me. Over time, we added four more people who represented different functions and levels within the organization. From a team standpoint, it was important that the team be somewhat small. Oftentimes, teams like this expand to a large size and get bogged down in a variety of details.

As stated earlier, I think it's best to build a small group focused on driving action, as this often leads to quicker and better results. It also ensures the team is focused on its main purpose, which is to implement and not get mired in trivial details and discussion.

As we began the training sessions, we focused on looking at ways to expand our recruiting pipelines. We created a list of organizations that could help us extend our reach into communities of color. As we met with these organizations and had them tour our facilities, we identified someone from their organization to regularly send new company job postings to. Foundationally, this helped us attract a demographic we'd left out in the past.

The second year of our efforts led to training our top leaders on how to create a better interview process that encourages an even playing field when hiring. We focused on how to identify and minimize unconscious bias from this key process. We also went through a second round of training for all employees. In this training, I asked participants to reflect on what they learned over the past year about themselves when it comes to racial diversity. The reflection and discussion led to a very rich time of sharing. It got many to think about a topic they had never reflected on. The purpose of this second training was to build more empathy and understanding around why there has been such a divide, where we are today, and what we can do about it in our own sphere of influence.

As I finish writing this book, we are now entering a phase where we're participating in a program geared to help us improve our hiring and selection process.[56] We're also feeling our way through a mentoring-type program for people of color in our organization that's proving fruitful. Our HR team is now reporting on metrics and developing a framework for how we can be more of a "trusted partner" to ethnically diverse organizations we're connecting with. Have we made progress? Yes! In the last year, the number of ethnically diverse employees in our organization has grown by 35%, new hires by 18.75%, and the number of candidates applying to our organization has grown by over 349%! Are we where we need to be? No, but we're laying a foundation that will increase our racial and ethnic makeup in the future.

Reflection

I feel like any multiethnic initiative needs to be labeled:

WARNING:
THERE WILL BE PUSHBACK!

Over the course of the two trainings, we received a largely positive response from our team. However, there were some individuals who didn't think the topic was appropriate and were quick to criticize. At times, people made comments that both hurt and bothered me.

I knew to expect this, but it still troubled me when it happened. Whenever challenging topics are discussed in the workplace, some people won't like it. Sometimes, it feels emotionally and socially costly. On the one hand, I look to learn from the feedback I receive. I've made some mistakes, and others have shared great insights, so I've adjusted accordingly. On the other hand, there are times when there's no practical benefit from the feedback. Oftentimes, it's just a different opinion. In this case, there's no reason to let the comments change what you're doing. Discussing feedback with those who are confidants is always helpful in sorting through how best to respond while not overreacting.

Although we're in the early stages of our multiethnic journey, there is a great foundation for growth being laid within the company. In general, most people are positive about our efforts. Our recruiting contacts and pipelines have expanded, and we're now working on the hiring and selection systems to help us gain greater traction in becoming a more diverse company. In reality, the hardest parts have been hearing a few people say critical things about the initiative and navigating any pushback. My hope is that you can see how—with intentional effort—you can make real change in your organization, too.

My Learnings

I want to close this chapter by sharing some of the key learnings and mistakes I made along the way. I want to be transparent with my thoughts and feelings as you might experience something similar. The more honest we are with ourselves, the more likely we are to learn and make progress. I've been doing this work for a long time, and I'm still learning how to do it well. It's important to remember not to require perfection from yourself or your plan as a criterion for whether it's successful. Great progress can't be made without making some mistakes. The key is that you learn from them.

What are some of my key learnings?

- I've overreacted to criticism, which led me down a path of self-pity, making me want to retreat and give up.

- I've learned to filter the feedback. I process and learn from what's shared, but I don't let the strong comments derail progress.

- I went too long before initiating a guiding team. Once I did, it provided more support and broadened my understanding of what needed to happen, making work on the initiative more sustainable.

- At first, our meetings were too infrequent, which slowed the pace of implementing good ideas. So, we changed them to a quarterly rhythm, which allowed us to gain better traction.

- From a training perspective, I've been given feedback that the conversation has been largely about blacks and whites and should include more discussion about other ethnic groups. Black people, along with Native Americans, have felt the greatest impact from historical practices, so it's a good place to start, but it's also true that other ethnic groups experience prejudice and bias in the workplace, so this should be shared as well.

- Although the training is focused on racial diversity, it's extremely important to point people to the broader issue of bias since this is easier for people to swallow and relate to as it covers all types of partiality.

- Early on, I didn't debrief enough with others. Part of this was due to being tired of criticism and also being afraid a new idea would take us in a direction that would slow progress.

- I've learned to acknowledge that I'm human and have feelings, too. This may sound obvious, but at times, I thought I could push past criticism and later realized I needed to deal with my feelings. Ultimately, I'm learning to deal with being vulnerable and not letting pushback cause me to give up or backtrack.

- This subject gets messy, and people's opinions are all over the place. I've learned that I need to take time to get away, collect my thoughts, and confide in those who care about me. Setting aside time to process my thoughts by myself as well as with those who care has been very helpful.

- All in all, I'm learning to be okay with the pain, misunderstanding, and tension that accompany this challenging subject. After all, it's part of the price to pay for moving an extremely important topic forward.

CHAPTER SEVEN

Key Insights for the Journey

Nothing is so terrible as activity without insight.
—Thomas Carlyle

A s I bring this book to a close, I'm going to briefly hit some key notes that are either worth repeating or that I haven't had a place to put previously. If you feel stuck in the course of implementing a multiethnic strategy, it may be helpful to peruse these insights as you navigate obstacles along the way.

Top-Leader Buy-in

I cannot emphasize enough that top leadership buy-in and ownership are critical for success. Change will happen more quickly if there's true "heart" transformation happening at the highest levels. This doesn't mean you can't make progress if there hasn't been this type of deep change, but it does mean other organizational issues will quickly push this aside if a leader's heart hasn't been impacted in some way.

White Leadership

Since most U.S. businesses are led by white people, they need to lead the charge in making this change. Several people of color have expressed to me that they're tired of talking about this issue and tired of trying to get white people to understand. Whites need to take responsibility and initiative and share in the burden of cultivating multiethnicity. The human tendency is to hold onto one's privileges and power, but we need to stop thinking about this as a zero-sum game. One person's gain doesn't mean another person's loss. In reality, you're making your organization more robust.

As a corollary to this, a couple of leaders who are people of color suggested to me that white people will listen to the conversation better when it comes from other whites. As a leader, you need to model what you want your employees to do. The bottom line is that those who lead the organization need to intentionally pursue multiethnicity, or it won't become a reality.

Tell the Whole Story

History is a great teacher. Incorporating the history of race in America (FHA guidelines, G.I. Bill, redlining...) into your training helps people understand the impact systemic racism (institutional and structural racism are similar terms) has had on our country. It helps people understand why we still have lingering effects today, which increases their likelihood of wanting to do something about it. As mentioned in chapter four, incorporating more recent history on this topic helps people understand the gravity of what's happened historically. Additionally, including company history along with local history (your city) is effective in making it more personal. It helps people see the problem within their context.

Celebrate People of Color Achievement

It's important to acknowledge people of color's positive contributions to our country when training on this topic. Not only have people of color been grossly discriminated against, but they have a long history of accomplishment and unwavering strength that all Americans should be proud of.

Set a Tone of Grace and Forgiveness

Grace and forgiveness should guide the tone for any discussion on this topic. Truth-telling must take place in an environment that is safe for all sides while bathed in grace and acceptance. A grace and forgiveness tone encourages

greater self-awareness, which can lead to personal transformation on this topic. Shaming people is ineffective and
unnecessary.

Draw White People into Conversation

People of color have a lot more thoughts and examples to
share on this topic than white people do. Whites have less
understanding of the issues and need to be drawn into the
conversation. The facilitator should set a tone of listening
respectfully on the one hand and sharing with vulnerability
on the other.

Lean on an Expert

Some leaders sincerely want to cultivate multiethnicity but
lack the know-how. It is very important to engage an inside
or outside coach and/or participate in an association or network to provide encouragement and guidance.

Stick to the Plan

Multiethnic initiatives can easily get pushed aside as the
demands of the organization increase. Following a clear plan
is essential for long-term progress. Remember, it's the right
thing to do and the cost is very low.

Get Creative

Developing creative ways to conduct your training, like putting on a short play that exposes the issue or some type of
race simulation (similar to a poverty simulation), can help
get the message across as it touches people's emotions.

Bring People Together

One of the best ways to eradicate racism and ignorance is for white people to spend time together with people of color. Building relationships across racial and ethnic lines breaks down barriers, increases empathy, and builds trust.

Provide Navigational Support

Several people of color—especially first and second-generation immigrants—have expressed to me that the biggest challenge they face is navigating our systems (jobs, education, access to capital, etc.). Knowing who and how best to network is crucial for making progress in our society.

Create Accountability

Fundamentally, moving in the direction of multiethnicity requires a solid change management plan to which top leaders are accountable.

Churches

The following are a few insights geared specifically toward church settings.

Remember the First Church

Learn from history. The name "Christian" was first given to those who were part of the early church in the city of Antioch, which is located in modern-day Turkey. What many don't realize is that the Antioch church was thriving and highly multiethnic.

Practice Ethnic Diversity

In the Bible, God makes it clear that there is only one race—the human race (Acts 17:26). At the same time, God designed humanity to be expressed through a variety of ethnicities. From the Old Testament to the New Testament, ethnic diversity is found throughout and embraced. In fact, the New Testament points us to a new humanity where all classes, genders, languages, cultures, and ethnicities are to function together as a witness to who the church is in representing Christ (Matt. 28:19; Acts 10:34-35; Gal. 3:28; Col. 3:11; Rev. 5:9, 7:9).

Highlight the Image of God

Focusing attention on the biblical concept of being created in the image of God will remind members that all people have inherent value and should be treated with dignity and respect (Gen. 1:27). Christians, of all people, should be at the forefront of promoting multiethnic equity and inclusion in the workplace.

Model Unity

In church settings, it is helpful to have white and person of color pastors/leaders jointly pray or discuss topics of racism together to serve as a visual reminder of unity around this topic.

Seek Integration, Not Assimilation

There is a tendency in churches (and many organizations) to move toward an assimilationist approach where the minority population takes on the culture of the majority. The alternative is an integrationist approach where preferences are given up on all sides for the sake of a unified body of Christ. Understand this tendency and look to move in a way that intentionally embraces all cultures (e.g., worship music, singing songs in a different language, etc.).

Present a Theology of Work

Incorporating a theology of work into the life of the church will help members see the connection between our faith and our work.[57] It also clarifies the importance of our calling to promote a healthy culture of multiethnic diversity in the workplace. What many don't understand is that all of our work (what we do, what we promote) matters to God. In fact, there's a sacredness to any work that we do.[58]

Inspire Your Community to Act

Churches can become a powerful witness to others if they handle multiethnicity well.[59] If the Church demonstrates multiethnic unity, it will inspire members of their community to make a difference in their respective organizations. Don't underestimate the power of this trickle-down effect.

Be Reconcilers

Many in the church were complicit in past practices of slavery and segregation,[60] and Christians are called to be ambassadors of reconciliation (2 Cor. 5:18-20). Reconciling in this context means acknowledging the past and seeking to restore what's broken while promoting harmony and unity across racial and ethnic divisions. Those who have been hurt by racism are encouraged to practice forgiveness. As Archbishop Desmond Tutu of South Africa reminds us in his profound book, there is "no future without forgiveness."[61]

Conclusion

You don't have to be great to start,
but you have to start to be great.
—Zig Zigler

Start from wherever you are and with whatever you've got.
—Jim Rohn

One day, three countertop installers representing Lumbermen's walked through the doors of that day's job. Two were African American, and one was white. The customer's job supervisor, likely thinking he was being clever and jovial, saw them and cried, "Here comes the dread crew!"

The two African American installers shrugged it off and got to work. Later, they said, "We're used to this. Another dumb comment from a white person." But a white installer, who had been through one of our trainings, recognized that it was not okay (it turned out this same supervisor had also made another derisive comment about race). He decided to do something out of the norm. Instead of letting it go, this installer called his supervisor to share what happened.

Eventually, these comments made their way to me. I decided to contact our customer's CEO and bring the incident to his attention. The result was that the CEO had a very frank conversation with the job supervisor, who admitted his wrongdoing. The CEO also told me he intended to share this situation with his entire leadership team to ensure learning took place across the organization. A simple step by one person to not let the comments go unnoticed led to organizational change. This is a great lesson in what my good friend and former HR executive, Ovell Barbee, often says, "Stop the silence!"[62]

This is what happens when you cultivate a healthy multiethnic organization. People stand up for one another as biases are exposed. This isn't about firing the individual who made the comment or even shaming them. It's about helping them correct the harmful biases that reside within so they can be part of building an organization where everyone belongs.

Do you want to make a difference in your organization? Do you want to increase the talent you bring into your organization and strengthen your culture? Do you want to see an organization that embodies all races and ethnicities? Do you want to be an organization that unleashes the power of being multiethnic?

If you're willing to pursue the principles laid out in this book, you'll experience this power. You'll find success in ways you never thought possible and realize a significant *advantage* when cultivating a multiethnic organization. You'll bring people together who've been historically separated. You'll encourage authentic healing to take place in people's hearts. You'll uplift all of humanity, and your organization will flourish in ways you never dreamed of!

Transformation happens when you intentionally work your plan over a long period of time. All you have to do is start. Just get started and watch the vision become a reality. The road may not be easy, but the cost is little. The road might be challenging, but the end result is fulfilling! We spend so much of our lives at work; why not use the workplace as an opportunity to bring people together for the common good? You have an opportunity to make a significant contribution to your organization as well as your community. It's the right thing to do and comes with so many benefits, so why not start the journey now?

Afterword

One day, you may be on the receiving end of strides made in this area as your family becomes more racially and ethnically diverse. The number of ethnically diverse marriages and relationships has grown substantially over the years. In fact, the term "sixth American" has been used to suggest that there are more than five distinct racial categories (Whites, Blacks, Hispanics, Asians, and Native Americans).[63] These sixth Americans live "a multiracial lifestyle with racially diverse friendship networks, employment settings, and integrated educational institutions."

Wouldn't it be uplifting if our children, grandchildren, and all future generations participated in organizations that understand the importance of this? Think of the legacy you'll leave your descendants. Your offspring will be the inheritors of what we're creating today. So, let's press forward in our efforts to become ethnically diverse. Yes, there truly is an *advantage* in a multiethnic organization!

SDG

Endnotes

1 Statista, U.S. share living in poverty by race and Hispanic origin in the United States from 1959 to 2022 (2023).
2 U.S. Census Bureau (2023).
3 Pew Research Center, The changing face of Congress in 8 charts, February 7, 2023.
4 McKay, Lisa Camner, "How the racial wealth gap has evolved-and why it persists." Federal Reserve Bank of Minneapolis, October 3, 2022. Accessed September 23, 2024. https://www.minneapolisfed.org/article/2022/how-the-racial-wealth-gap-has-evolved-and-why-it-persists
5 U.S. Bureau of Labor Statistics, (2023).
6 U.S. Census Bureau, (n.d.).
7 U.S. Census Bureau quickfacts: United States, accessed May 29, 2024, https://www.census.gov/quickfacts/fact/table/US/PST045219.
8 Survey: "8 Facts about love and marriage in America." Pew Research Center analysis of 2008-2015 American Community Survey and 1980 decennial census (IPUMS), February 13, 2019. Accessed July 4, 2023. www.pewresearch.org/short-reads/2019/02/13/8-facts-about-love-and-marriage.

9   Angelou, Maya. *I Know Why the Caged Bird Sings*. New York, NY: Random House, 1969, ix.

10 Case Study: "How Mercy Health reduced the impact of bias in the hiring process: Standardized assessments yield more diverse hires." Published in Advisory Board, July 29, 2020.

11 Sinek, Simon. *Start With WHY: How Great Leaders Inspire Everyone to Take Action*. New York, NY: Penguin Group, 2009.

12 Arana, Marie. *LatinoLand: A Portrait of America's Largest and Least Understood Minority*. New York, NY: Simon & Schuster, 2024.

13 Rock, David, and Grant, Heidi. "Diversity And Inclusion: Why Diverse Teams Are Smarter." Harvard Business Review, November 4, 2016. Accessed on July 4, 2023. hbr.org/2016/11/why-diverse-teams-are-smarter.

14 Ng, E.S., & Sears, G.J., "Walking the Talk on Diversity: CEO Beliefs, Moral Values, and the Implementation of Workplace Diversity Practices." Journal of Business Ethics, 2018, 437-450.

15 1619 is the year of the first recorded trade of Africans for supplies in Virginia.

16 Shenvi, Neil & Sawyer, Pat. Critical Dilemma: The Rise of Critical Theories and Social Justice Ideology – Implications for the Church and Society. Eugene, Oregon: Harvest House Publishers, 2023, 211.

17 McChesney, Chris, Covey, Sean, & Huling, Jim. *The Four Disciplines of Execution: Achieving Your Wildly Important Goals*. New York, NY: Simon & Schuster Paperbacks, 2012.

18 Ackerman-Anderson, L. & Anderson, D. *The Change Leader's Roadmap: How to Navigate Your Organization's transformation*. San Francisco, CA: Pfeiffer, 2010.

19 Kotter, John. *Leading Change*. Boston, MA: Harvard Business Review Press, 2012.

20 Ackerman-Anderson, L. & Anderson, D. *Beyond Change Management: How to Achieve Breakthrough Results Through Conscious Change Leadership*. San Francisco: CA. Pfeiffer, 2010.

21 David A. Garvin and Michael A. Roberto. *HBR's 10 Must Reads on Change Management*. Boston, MA: Harvard Business School Publishing Corporation, 2011.

22 Kotter, John. Leading Change. Boston, MA: Harvard Business Review Press, 2012, 21.

23 Cashman, Kevin. *Leadership From the Inside Out: Becoming a Leader for Life*. Oakland, CA: Berrett-Koehler Publishers, Inc., 1998.

24 Poutiatine, M.I., "What is transformation? Nine Principles Toward an Understanding Transformational Process for Transformational Leadership." Journal of Transformative Education, 2009, 189-208.

25 Massie, Victoria M., "White women benefit most from affirmative action – and are among its fiercest opponents." Vox, May 25, 2016. www.vox.com/2016/5/25/11682950/fisher-supreme-court-white-women-affirmative-action.

26 The Indian Removal Act was signed into law by President Andrew Jackson on May 28, 1830, authorizing the president to grant lands west of the Mississippi in exchange for Indian lands within existing state borders. A few tribes went peacefully, but many resisted the relocation policy. During the fall and winter of 1838 and 1839, the Cherokees were forcibly moved west by the United States government. Approximately 4,000 Cherokees died on this forced march, which became known as the "Trail of Tears."

27 The Change Curve is based on a model of the five stages of grief – denial, anger, bargaining, depression and acceptance – originally described by Elisabeth Kubler-Ross in her 1969 book *On Death and Dying*.

28 Critical Race Theory (Britanica definition) is an off shoot of Critical Theory and holds that racism is inherent in the law and legal institutions of the United States. Critical race theorists are generally dedicated to applying their understanding of the institutional or structural nature of racism to the concrete (if distant) goal of eliminating all race-based and other unjust hierarchies.

29 Kotter, John P. "Leading Change: Why Transformation Efforts Fail." Harvard Business Review, May-June 1995. Accessed July 4, 2023. hbr.org/1995/05/leading-change-why-transformation-efforts-fail-2.

30 Mangena, Daniel. "Why the 10-80-10 Rule Is Key To Achieving Success." LifeHack, November 29.2021. www.lifehack.org/913626/10-80-10-rule.

31 Dweck, Carol S. *Mindset: The New Psychology of Success. How We Can Learn to Fulfill Our Potential*. New York, NY: Ballantine Books, 2016, 46.

32 Eberhardt, Jennifer. *BIASED: Uncovering the Hidden Prejudice That Shapes What We See, Think, and Do*. New York, NY: Penguin Books, 2019, 33.

33 Advisory Board. "Case Study: How Mercy Health reduced the impact of bias in the hiring process." July 29, 2020. (Advisory Board was founded in 1979 to highlight the best thinking in healthcare.)

34 Advisory Board. "Case Study: How Mercy Health reduced the impact of bias in the hiring process." July 29, 2020.

35 Eberhardt, Jennifer. BIASED: *Uncovering the Hidden Prejudice That Shapes What We See, Think, and Do*. New York, NY: Penguin Books, 2019, 269-270.

36 Cain Miller, Claire and Katz, Josh, "What Researchers Discovered When They Sent 80,000 Fake Resumes to U.S. Jobs." N.Y. Times, April 8, 2024.

37 Cooperrider, David L and Whitney, Diana. *Appreciative Inquiry: A Positive Revolution in Change*. Oakland, CA: Berrett-Koehler Publishers, 2005.

38 Visit the Black Lives Matter website (https:// blacklivesmatter.com) to better understand the movement's purpose.

39 Critical Race Theory (Britanica definition) is an off shoot of Critical Theory and holds that racism is inherent in the law and legal institutions of the United States. Critical race theorists are generally dedicated to applying their understanding of the institutional or structural nature of racism to the concrete (if distant) goal of eliminating all race-based and other unjust hierarchies.

40 Guynn, Jessica. "Affirmative action wars hit the workplace: Conservatives target 'woke' DEI programs." USA Today, September 15, 2023.

41 Eberhardt, Jennifer. BIASED: *Uncovering the Hidden Prejudice That Shapes What We See, Think, and Do*. New York, NY: Penguin Books, 2019, 39.

42 Brown, Brene'. *Rising Strong: How the Ability to Reset Transforms the Way We Live, Love, Parent and Lead*. New York, NY: Random House, 2015.

43 Singal, Jesse. "Diversity Trainings Try to Change Hearts and Minds. That's a Mistake." N.Y. Times Opinion section, January 17, 2023.

44 Banaji, Mahzarin and Dobbin, Frank. "Why DEI Training Doesn't Work – and How to Fix It." The Wall Street Journal, September 17, 2023.

45 Eberhardt, Jennifer. *Biased: Uncovering the Hidden Prejudice That Shapes What We See, Think, and Do.* New York, NY: Penguin Books, 2019, 301.

46 https://en.wikipedia.org/wiki/Killing_of_Patrick_Lyoya

47 Christopher Columbus Journal. The American Yawp. Accessed on July 4, 2023. www.americanyawp.com/reader/the-new-world/journal-of-christopher-columbus.

48 Shenvi, Neil & Sawyer, Pat. *Critical Dilemma: The Rise of Critical Theories and Social Justice Ideology – Implications for the Church and Society.* Eugene, Oregon: Harvest House Publishers, 2023, 213-216.

49 Prewitt, Kenneth. "Racial Classification in America." Daedalus, Winter, 2005. Accessed July 4, 2023. www.amacad.org/publication/racial-classification-america.

50 No author listed. "Reconstruction vs. Redemption." National Endowment for the Humanities, February 11, 2014. Accessed July 4, 2023. www.neh.gov/news/reconstruction-vs-redemption.

51 No author listed. "Housing Inequity, In Black And White." Mortgage Banker Magazine, January 2022 issue. Accessed on July 4, 2023. nationalmortgageprofessional.com/news/housing-inequity-black-and-white.

52 "Responses Coming from the Civil Rights Movement," PBS, accessed September 26, 2024, https://www.pbs.org/wgbh/americanexperience/features/eyesontheprize-responses-coming-civil-rights-movement/.

53 As an example: Robinson, Todd E. *A CITY WITHIN A CITY: The Black Freedom Struggle in Grand Rapids, Michigan.* Philadelphia, PA: Temple University Press, 2013.

54 Thiel, Peter. *Zero to One: Notes On Startups, Or How To Build The Future.* New York, NY: Crown Business, 2014.

55 Kotkin, Joel, "The cities where African-Americans are doing the best economically." Forbes, January 15, 2015. Accessed on July 4, 2023. www.forbes.com/sites/joelkotkin/2015/01/15/the-cities-where-african-americans-are-doing-the-best-economically/?sh=174887b9164f.

56 Hire Reach Academy is a five-month virtual academy program that gives participating organizations the tools and knowledge they need to create a skills-based hiring process. You can learn more about Hire Reach by accessing their website: www.hirereach.org/academy.

57 Four Sources to Explore Further: https://www.theologyofwork.org/; https://www.thegospelcoalition.org/topics/faith-and-work/; https://faithandwork.com/; https://www.madetoflourish.org/

58 Raynor, Jordan. *The Sacredness of Secular Work: 4 Ways Your Job Matters for Eternity (Even When You're Not Sharing the Gospel).* Colorado Springs, CO: WaterBrook, 2024.

59 Shenvi, Neil & Sawyer, Pat. Critical Dilemma: The Rise of Critical Theories and Social Justice Ideology – Implications for the Church and Society. Eugene, Oregon: Harvest House Publishers, 2023, 477.

60 Tisby, Jemar. *The COLOR of COMPROMISE: The truth about the American Church's complicity in racism.* Grand Rapids, MI: Zondervan Reflective, 2019

61 Tutu, Desmond. *No Future Without Forgiveness.* New York NY: Doubleday, 1999.

62 Barbee, Ovell. *THE BIG HOUSE: A Human-Centered & Progressive Approach to DEI and Positive Workforce Engagement.* Baltimore, MD: Publish Your Gift, 2023, 85.

63 Yancey, George, *Beyond Racial Division: A Unifying Alternative To Colorblindness And Antiracism.* Downers Grove, IL: InterVarsity Press, 2022, 159.

Acknowledgments

I am extremely grateful to all whom I've had the pleasure of discussing this topic with: Dr. Brad Smith and Dr. Bryan McCabe of Bakke Graduate University, without whose dissertation encouragement and guidance this book wouldn't have been possible. I can't say enough about Steve Petersen (Lumbermen's, Inc. President), who gave his full support and allowed much of my research findings to become a reality in the workplace.

In crafting this book, Fred Keller and Julie McFarland freely gave their time to offer important insights and experiences shared in this book. To Steve Sanders, Brad Vernier, and Ovell Barbee, thank you for offering insightful feedback during the rough draft stage.

Thank you, Paul Cooper, for being a tremendous friend and confidant. My heart goes out to Artie Lindsay, Kizombo Kalumbula, Jr., and the wonderful community of Tabernacle Community Church, who seek to live out the multiethnic vision of the church. I'd also like to thank my great friend Pete Knibbe, along with Kevin Suraj, Andy Hunt, Willy Kotiuga, Cisco Gonzalez, Jim Hackett, Marylu Villarreal, Elsa Sanchez, Humberto Ramirez, Edward Rhetta, Al Erisman, Rocky Duran, Julian Newman, and Tony Martin for their important feedback.

I'm grateful to all who participated in my dissertation interviews who haven't been named: Angela Nelson, Bill Guest, Bob Krestakos, Cle Jackson, Daniel Williams, Dave Barrett, Dave Beelen, Dr. Justin Beene, Isabel Medellin, Joe Jones, John Girgis, Kenyatta Brame, Kyle Ray, Marvin Williams, Rick DeHaan, Wayman Britt, and Will Osmun.

I'm also so thankful for all of my teammates on the Lumbermen's Racial Diversity team who helped shape and implement these ideas in our place of work. Thank you, David Haigler, Henry Bouma, Janae Flowers, Jill Carroll, Laura Longstreet, Lee Figures, Olivia Martinelli, and Tank Johnson!

I'd also be remiss if I didn't thank all those (too many to name) who participated in the focus groups and trainings I've conducted, as their honest thoughts and comments impacted this work.

Last but not least, I'd like to thank the Ethos Collective team, with special thanks to Brad Fuhauff for content editing, along with Dana Lyons and Travis White for their encouragement and project management support. And special thanks to Denise Williams for her comprehensive editing and insight that led to the final draft—thank you so much!

About the Author

Kevin Heyne grew up in a variety of diverse settings on the East Coast (Philadelphia, Washington DC, and New York City metropolitan areas), where he attended highly multiethnic schools and eventually settled in Grand Rapids, Michigan.

Over the last thirty years, Kevin has held a variety of leadership and executive positions in the corporate and non-profit sectors. Most recently, he held a high-level role for a Fortune 1000 global company and was part of a global leadership team. Currently, Kevin serves as an executive for a highly successful Midwest manufacturer and distributor of Building Materials products, where he's implementing the ideas in this book.

Kevin is married with three children. Kevin recently earned a Doctorate of Transformational Leadership (DTL) with an emphasis on Entrepreneurial Organizational Transformation. Kevin is also an ordained associate teaching pastor of a local multiethnic church and co-founder of Transformational Executive Coaching (TEC). TEC is a consulting-training organization that brings people together from diverse ethnic and racial backgrounds with the intent of developing better executives and transformational leaders who impact their organizations and communities for the common good.

DO YOU WANT YOUR ORGANIZATION TO REACH ITS FULL POTENTIAL?

MultiEthnicAdvantage.com

Dr. Kevin Heyne is available for select speaking engagements. To learn more about this, visit our website.

THIS BOOK IS PROTECTED INTELLECTUAL PROPERTY

Instant IP ™

The author of this book values Intellectual Property and has utilized Instant IP, a groundbreaking technology.
Instant IP is the patented, blockchain-based solution for Intellectual Property protection.

Blockchain is a distributed public digital record that can not be edited. Instant IP timestamps the author's ideas, creating a smart contract, thus an immutable digital asset that proves ownership and establishes a first to use / first to file event.

Protected by Instant IP ™

LEARN MORE AT INSTANTIP.TODAY